PRAISE FOR
WATER ON FIRE

"*Water on Fire* is not a common story of war, loss, displacement, and identity crises, as much as it is a way to trace their inheritance. Tarek El-Ariss tells us that 'cutting' and 'storytelling' are the same word in Arabic (*qass*), and discovers that the impossibility of mourning cannot be reconciled through mere descriptive remembering of events. Rather, this reconciliation demands recalling images and fictional characters from scattered books, where literature can make reality of geography, disorder, and vulnerability."
— Iman Mersal, author of *The Threshold: Poems*

"In this beautifully written book, Tarek El-Ariss takes his readers on a journey of discovery of one's identity, commitment to humanity, and sorrows and ambitions, drawing a vivid picture of life at war from Beirut to New York. A must-read book!"
— Alaa Al Aswany, author of *The Yacoubian Building*

ALSO BY TAREK EL-ARISS

Trials of Arab Modernity: Literary Affects and the New Political

Leaks, Hacks, and Scandals: Arab Culture in the Digital Age

*The Arab Renaissance: A Bilingual Anthology
of the* Nahda (editor)

WATER

on

FIRE

A Memoir of War

Tarek El-Ariss

OTHER PRESS / NEW YORK

The author would like to thank the John Simon
Guggenheim Memorial Foundation for the fellowship
that allowed him to write this book.

An earlier version of Chapter 2: The Beachcombers was
published in *Di'van: A Journal of Accounts*, 34–43, University of
New South Wales Faculty of Art & Design, 2018.

Production editor: Yvonne E. Cárdenas
Text designer: Jennifer Daddio
This book was set in Bembo and Veneer
by Alpha Design & Composition of Pittsfield, NH

1 3 5 7 9 10 8 6 4 2

Library of Congress Cataloging-in-Publication Data
Names: El-Ariss, Tarek, author.
Title: Water on fire : a memoir of war / Tarek El-Ariss.
Description: New York : Other Press, [2024]
Identifiers: LCCN 2023038898 (print) | LCCN 2023038899 (ebook) |
ISBN 9781635424461 (paperback) | ISBN 9781635424478 (ebook)
Subjects: LCSH: El-Ariss, Tarek. | Lebanon—History—Civil War,
1975-1990—Personal narratives, Lebanese. | Lebanon—History—
Civil War, 1975-1990—Children. | Lebanese Americans—Biography. |
Middle East specialists—United States—Biography.
Classification: LCC DS87.2.E43 A3 2024 (print) |
LCC DS87.2.E43 (ebook) | DDC 956.9204/4092 [B]—dc23/eng/20231213
LC record available at https://lccn.loc.gov/2023038898
LC ebook record available at https://lccn.loc.gov/2023038899

Disclaimer: I have omitted the names of certain individuals to
protect their privacy. And although this is a work of nonfiction
that deals with personal experiences and historical events, memory
and storytelling often blur the distinction between fiction and
reality, especially from the perspective of a child.

Job got up and tore his robe and shaved his head.
Then he fell to the ground in worship
and said: "Naked I came from my mother's
womb, and naked I will depart."

—THE BOOK OF JOB

Be like water, my friend.

—BRUCE LEE

1

WEST END BOY

It was the afternoon of a cold spring day. I entered a building lobby on the Upper West Side and headed straight to the left, just as I was instructed. I looked for the name on an intercom by a large brass door. It was the second one from the top. I pressed the button and was immediately buzzed in.

The door led to a windowless room with a couple of couches and chairs, and a stack of magazines on a coffee table, including *New York* and *The New Yorker*. The room had old brown carpeting, thinned out by all the wet boots that had rubbed against it over the years. The occasional steaming to remove salt and stain had further shaved off layers of the carpet. There was also a closet with a few coats on the rack and some school bags on the floor. On the wall hung framed posters of classical music concerts and art exhibits. I want to say that Matisse's painting *Dance (I)*—the one at MoMA—was among them, but I don't think it was.

Waiting in the room that day was a woman with graying hair and round glasses whom I would see at the same spot and at the same time for years to come. This new companion and I never uttered a word. Furtive smiles timidly exchanged in a dark waiting room expressed solidarity on our respective journeys into the origin of the self.

After I waited a few minutes, a door opened and another woman appeared. She was in her midfifties and had curly brown hair and hazel eyes that said it all. She was my therapist. She looked me in the eyes as she called my name, inviting me to come into her office.

Between the waiting room and the therapists' offices there was a narrow hallway that led to an exit door. The patients entered and exited from two different doors, minimizing the chances of running into people they knew.

A conspicuous object on the floor was an old white-noise machine, right outside my therapist's door. The machine was humming like an open faucet with no water, ensuring that whoever went by that door was not likely to hear what was being revealed inside.

My therapist's office was small but bright, with a big window overlooking West End Avenue. The furniture dated back to the eighties. There was a bookshelf on the left, a blue corduroy couch or chaise longue on the right, and a large Caucasian rug adorning the floor. The therapist sat on an old Eames chair with a stool in front of her and a framed certificate from the New York Freudian Society above her head. A couple of paintings were hung on the walls, one of them depicting an open door that leads to a dark room at the end of a long, narrow hallway.

The therapist I went to see that day was no ordinary one. She was a psychoanalyst in the great tradition of Sigmund Freud, who identified the unconscious and the portals we enter to revisit the past and heal the present. His discoveries include repression, displacement, and projection—concepts and words that entered everyday language and popularized talk therapy as we know it.

But few are the therapists today who adhere to the healing model that Freud put in place. Those who do, meet with their patients four times a week for the duration of the analysis, which could take years. Mine lasted eight. Eight long years of riding subways and ringing bells and talking—and talking and talking—and journeying into the past to recover a feeling, an impression, a whisper. Every session transformed that blue couch in a therapist's office on the Upper West Side into a launchpad for a monstrous drill that burrowed in my psyche like a Jules Verne machine.

Freud had been in my life from the minute I awakened to this world. I remember when my brother stormed into my dad's room one day and emphatically declared his opposition to the fact that I was sleeping with my mom in the same bed. Having read something about the Oedipus complex, he explained to my dad—who had read Freud as well—how dangerous intimacies could affect a child's development.

A blurry scene comes to mind. I'm in that room as well, standing to the side of my dad's pink couch, where he loved to recline, Roman style. Shadows of my animated brother practicing his dangerous knowledge unravel like screens in my mind. That day, my brother read something that allowed him to see the future. And like Cassandra in Greek mythology, he became consumed by a vision of blood and fire.

> *Oh, misery, misery! Again comes on me*
> *The terrible labor of true prophecy, dizzying prelude.*
> *Do you see these who sit before the house,*
> *Children, like the shapes of dreams?*
> *Children who seem to have been killed by their*
>   *kinsfolk,*
> *Filling their hands with meat, flesh of themselves,*
> *Guts and entrails, handfuls of lament—*
> *Clear what they hold - the same their father tasted.*

As I came of age and started confronting crises of identity and desire, I, too, turned to Freud and his interpretation of Greek myth and literature. Before I even stepped foot in my analyst's office, I was already practicing Freud's dicta left and right, applying them to myself, to those around me, and to the novels and films I was reading and watching.

At that time, I considered Freud's theory to be foolproof, capable of explaining anything and everything under the sun, including individual and collective behaviors. People repressed and acted out, nations fantasized about prehistoric origins and sought to recuperate them through a return to the womb. Projection here and displacement there, Freud was the organizer that gave meaning to the fragmented world that I had come from and that was chasing me wherever I went.

Apply Freud and you will heal!

Moving to New York City after several years of living in upstate New York, where I underwent grueling graduate training in the humanities and in Freud's theories specifically, I was experiencing burnout. I had no idea what I was going through at first, but I found myself fighting with everyone and suffering from inexplicable rashes and breakdowns. Something was wrong, but I couldn't diagnose it myself. I needed help, another reader of Freud perhaps, who could immediately recognize my symptoms and show me how to heal them. I was looking for an interlocutor who would give me a few pointers and help me adjust to New York and its demanding lifestyle.

I got a recommendation for a psychoanalyst on the Upper West Side and went to see her with family pictures in one hand and teenage poetry in the other. I went equipped with evidence that traveled in tightly packed suitcases from Lebanon to Africa, and from upstate to New York City. I was like those art experts who bring drawings to consult a colleague about their provenance and authenticity. I needed a second opinion, nothing more. I knew how and why I fit into the theory that the great master had developed. I just needed her to confirm a few things and recommend a treatment. I needed another set of eyes.

The more I reflect on that first encounter with my analyst in March 2001, the more I see myself as one of those asylum seekers who carry evidence of their abuse, desperate to convince a case worker of the legitimacy of their claim. Documents detailing torture needed to be seen to be believed. This refugee came to indict abusers from the past. He came to seek protection from the demons that were chasing him everywhere, at night. He came to make sure that their tentacles could never reach him in his newfound land.

Except my documents were poems written in French about teenage angst, and family photos, mostly of my mom and a few of my dad. The pictures showed a happy family with a bit too much affection, perhaps. Two pictures stand out: one of me and my mom, like a prince and a queen, all in white. We are sitting on a beige silk couch with our arms stretched out, touching in the middle. Another picture is of the entire family on the terrace, with me lying on my dad's lap like I would lie on that blue couch in my analyst's office for the next eight years.

I brought these pictures to show her something about the poses and the proximity that my brother had warned about. She needed to see it so she could fix me, put me back together, and erect that boundary that should have been there from the beginning. I presented the evidence and explained to her that I, too, grew up in a traditional bourgeois household, with a nanny and a stay-at-home mom, much like Freud's patients. I said:

"I come from the nineteenth century."

She looked perplexed and immediately replied:

"I thought you were from Beirut. Don't you want to talk about the war?"

2

THE BEACHCOMBERS

Beirut is a city that goes into the sea, which envelops and contains it. Its coast is rugged, modern, protruding into nature. Beirutis push the sea away like they push an overbearing mother. They claim their space and assert their independence by dumping garbage and pouring concrete. And the sea hits back by cradling foreign fleets that bring bombs and bondage.

The sea of Beirut disguises fire beneath every wave, a combustion with every ebbing, spoken in different tongues. This incendiary sea tortures Beirutis with lamentations over exiled lovers and outlaws seeking other shores. The sea drowns them in tears, sparking their desire to join those who departed and to disappear with them beyond the horizon, never to resurface.

Yet Beirutis find ways to reconcile with the sea. Their coastline is home to private beach clubs nestled at the foot of rocky cliffs. For many Beirutis living through the 1975–90 civil war, these beach clubs became their only outlets during months and years of siege and enclosure. Their patrons withstood the war by playing a dangerous game—a forbidden game—in the sun. These fearless beachgoers risked the lives of their children for a swim, a tan, and a short drive to the beach. Their actions were a perverse affront to war.

But what valuables were these Beirutis searching for by going to the beach every day, from May to October, from morning to evening? What meaning were they seeking by choosing to cohabit with war? The answer might be found by accessing a portal that opened in a therapist's office on the Upper West Side, and through a red hole in the head of a handsome youth called Ahmad.

When one thinks of Mediterranean beaches, one imagines France's Côte d'Azur or the Greek isles. These beaches have captured people's imagination and inspired dreams and fantasies of all kinds. In the film *Summer Lovers*, young men and women dive into Santorini's blue sea, blissful and full of wonders. In Alexandria, the iconic Stanley Beach was immortalized in Youssef Chahine's film *Alexandria . . . Why?*, recalling the city of his youth, a melting pot of Arabs and Europeans, Muslims, Christians, and Jews. Menaced by World War II, these Alexandrians came together at the beach, fishing, swimming, and flirting on the Corniche, which stretches for miles. Chahine blends sea and war to portray his own Alexandria, accessing it through special currents and tides that go in and out of rock constellations strewn along the coast.

Beirut, farther north and east along the coast from Alexandria, boasts a vibrant beach culture of its own, where people swim and snorkel, play backgammon and *palettes* (beach racquetball). This culture can be traced back to the nineteenth century and such beach cafés as Hajj Dawood. One of the last survivors of these traditional cafés is Rawda, also known as Shatila, which continues to attract families, artists, and tourists in search of a bygone era.

The coast is so much a part of Beirut's identity that a mere rock formation has become its icon. Like Paris's Eiffel Tower or New York's Statue of Liberty, Raouche's Pigeon Rock figures on its country's currency, affirming the city's attachment to its rocky shore.

By the fifties and sixties, there appeared a cast of simple beach clubs—Long Beach and Sporting Club among them—poured with concrete, adorning Beirut's coastline. By the late seventies, such beach resorts as Summerland were built on the southern outskirts of the city, introducing a glitzy model with nightclubs, restaurants, and tennis courts. Gloria Gaynor sang at Summerland in 1980. That night, my parents were getting ready to attend the concert as the Israeli Air

Force, it was rumored, were preparing to bomb the Palestinian refugee camps across from the posh venue.

The war gradually infiltrated Beirut's beaches. When the city was divided in 1975, the beaches that survived were on the west side of the demarcation line. One of the first battles revolved around a cluster of beachfront hotels and became known as the Hotels War—it's vividly described in Ghada al-Samman's novel *Beirut Nightmares*. Despite the destruction, some beach clubs, like the Saint George, remained open, flaunting their bombed-out shells.

The war raided Beirut's beaches but couldn't wipe them out. In fact, the war turned them into the only outlet for those trapped in a city encircled by war and deprived of greenery. Beirutis flocked to these beaches not for the glamour they provided but to attenuate the toll of war. Going to the beach became an act of survival, an act of creation, in a city where the social fabric was disintegrating because of a violent conflict that would last fifteen years. For many, the beach was the last stand against an ever-tightening noose.

During the civil war, my family decided to stay and fight on. My father, who had studied and lived in the U.S., was never going to leave Beirut again. Perhaps he was afraid to leave, like the father in Ziad Doueiri's film *West Beirut*. During the Israeli invasion in 1982, my father was proud of being one of only seven physicians who kept his hospital running, performing all kinds of surgeries. He stayed put and rebuilt every time his practice got damaged from a missile hit or a car bomb. And when his work came to a grinding halt, he sold his inheritance and spent all his savings to provide for us.

We continued to go to school, however intermittently, throughout the protracted conflict. Dinners and parties were a staple of our life at war. Crossing checkpoints to visit friends and family in the East or traveling to Syria or Cyprus to catch a plane when Beirut's airport had shut down, we defied the water, electricity, and fuel shortages and confronted violence with illusory courage and obstinate joie de vivre.

In retrospect, I wonder if we shouldn't have stayed. Surviving the way we did forced us to suppress fear My father always reminded us that we were the courageous ones. We never went into the shelter, no matter how close the bombs fell; we stopped militiamen from squatting in empty apartments in our building; and we flouted shortages by buying water, which we'd store in the kitchen, the attic, and, once, in the bathtub. We stocked food and toothpaste, detergent and spices. During one of the worst episodes of the war, my father bought dozens of Perrier bottles and cans of boiled potatoes, which were all that was left at the only supermarket he found open that day. I remember witnessing the shopping bags that revealed the strange food items that were to be incorporated into our war diet.

We found a way to live around war, on its side, at its limits, in between bombs and abductions, fuel and power shortages. And we had the sea and the privileges of those Beirutis who could go to the beach every day, especially when work was slow and school was closed.

My father, who passed away suddenly in 1987, went to his clinic from nine to one most days. Before leaving work, he would call me—when the phones worked, that is—asking if he should pass by the house and take me to the beach or if I was going to ride with my mother.

By the end of the summer, we were freakishly tanned. People had different recipes for tanning oils, some involving Pepsi and beer, others peroxide and Mercurochrome (merbromin). We also had the iconic Ambre Solaire, which gave way to Lancaster, a potent tanning paste that left a bronze hue on new skin. Being white during the summer was an anomaly, a disease, a sign of staying in and capitulating to war's violence. When the beach season started, my mother and sister used to sit in an isolated location all the way at the end, by the rocks, ashamed of their whiteness. It was only when they got some color that they would join the rest of their friends and become like everyone else, equal under the sun.

At the beach, I fished, snorkeled, and collected seashells for my sister, who used to display them on a little blue table by her bedside. I made the dough we used for fish bait—yes, I used dough—melting butter and mixing it with flour and water. I spent hours fishing. I was alone in my world, at my designated spot. I would mostly catch small fish called *mwasta* (marbled spinefoot), which used to sting my fingers when I took them off the hook. At the end of the day, I would bring home my fish, insisting on cleaning and cooking them myself. I would cut their little bellies with my mother's cuticle scissors and then fry them in a kitchen that was dimly lit by a *lux* (camping lantern), due to power cuts.

The beach was no longer only a site of leisure and recreation but a space for inventing a reality adjacent to that of war. This new reality, however, came at a great price. How many times did we have to pack and rush home when the situation suddenly deteriorated? How many times did we endure the sounds of explosions, pretending they were too far away? Though we put on new skins and masks of courage, we were exposed, naked in our vulnerability, desperate to be together. So we played and gossiped and flirted in the sun.

We used to swim in the *piscine naturelle*, also known as *crique el-moj*, which was a pool-like cove that had a current effect, sucking us in and out. It was for the bold kids, the good swimmers, who would dive in to catch the wave, only to reemerge with cuts and bruises.

Our glittery bay that eyed the horizon, trapped between water and fire, provided us with the illusion of freedom. It made us carefree, alive, boisterous, and courageous in ways that we were not and could no longer be on the outside. So we tanned and groomed and snorkeled. These activities were not just an escape from war but rather a quest for something valuable that was lost and needed to be found, reinvented, ever so gently, every day.

We were like beachcombers, searching for valuable objects on the shore.

Looking back, combing surrounded us on all sides, giving new meaning to our daily rituals in the sun. I distinctly remember a famous nightclub at the Coral Beach Hotel, the Beachcomber, where people danced and drank Jamaica cocktails throughout the conflict.

In the language of war, combing designates a military operation that cleanses areas of rebels and intruders. As for *musht* (comb), in the Lebanese dialect it refers to the machine gun's magazine, full of tightly stacked bullets that fly hysterically in all directions. The sound of bullets used to lull me to sleep during the war. They were like a lullaby that a mother sings while caressing her child's hair.

Combing also means to render the hair orderly. It is the morning ritual that inaugurates the day, announcing its beginning and setting its rhythm. One of the first tools available to humankind, the comb neutralizes disorder, stemming through continuous and methodical movements the parasitic and the unwanted. With every stroke, the comb excludes the louse, the foreign, and what's outside. Combing is a form of weeding, a resistance against scavenging plants trying to take over the lawn, the garden, the beach at the edge of the city, which we cultivated daily with much love and great diligence. The comb's repetitive pulling on the hair, from the root out, straightens, organizes, and eliminates anxiety.

Oh comber comb her hair
Gently gently and don't cause her pain,
For she is a noble girl
Who's used to pampering.

In this traditional lullaby, which is sung for the bride on her wedding day, combing reveals the pain caused from breaking apart the embracing curls, intertwined in tiny knots. This is the pain of separation as the girl readies to leave home. Combing allays the girl's anxiety by reaffirming the familiar, re-creating home, our home at the beach during the war.

Fishing, swimming, and tanning are the kinds of combing we performed during this time. Other species practice combing or grooming as well. Monkeys and gorillas, our close kin, groom not only to delouse but also to express loyalty, love, affection, remorse, and distress.

Our combing and grooming in a war-ravaged city allowed us to restore a social bond that belonged to a different time, a different species. They allowed us to restart civilization, building it anew around swimming, tanning, and fishing. From this vulnerable space, where bodies were exposed to the sun and to the stray bullets of Lebanon's civil war, a new community arose through daily practices of intimacy.

There are several sayings by the Prophet Muhammad about combing that come to mind as well. In one saying, the Muslim community is compared to the comb's teeth: "From the time of Adam to this day humans have been created equal like the teeth of a comb, with no advantage for the Arab over the non-Arab, the red-skinned over the black, except in their piety."

In this saying, the comb is a model for equality, diversity, and intimacy. The comb confronts discrimination based on race and ethnicity, and sectarian and political divisions that consumed the Lebanese during the war. The comb, which has the power to separate and exclude, could also bring people together while recognizing their differences and vulnerabilities. Beirut's beachcombers survived war and divisions as God had created them, equal, laid bare in the sun.

In another saying, the Prophet aligns combing with smelling and remembering in a liminal state between life and death, between heaven and earth. On his nocturnal journey to heaven (*isra'*), the Prophet remembers smelling a sweet fragrance and asking the angel Gabriel about its provenance. Gabriel replied that it belongs to the comber of Pharaoh's daughter. This woman revealed her true faith when the iron comb dropped from her hand and she exclaimed, "In the Name of God!" (*bismillah*). When her mistress heard her, she inquired about the woman's faith and whether she believed in a god other than Pharaoh. As the comber proclaimed her belief in the true god, she was thrown into the fire.

The dropping of the comb exposes the comber's identity and transports her to heaven, where the Prophet smells her fragrance, learns of her story, and relays it to the believers. Combing thus describes the work of memory, of remembering what the Prophet said and experienced on his journey. It's also the recounting of episodes, anecdotes, and encounters by sifting through the past in a state of vulnerability

Today, my comb has dropped as well, uncovering a lost world that continues to live inside me. The beach life we invented in the midst of war is a landscape drawn by a painter through successive brushstrokes, cajoling the canvas, the screen, the scene of writing my war experience.

The movement of water going in and out of rocky clusters regulates the movement of memory. With every wave and every bubble forming at the surface, this movement uncovers new images, old ones. The foam that kids like me used to re-create in their bathtubs with bubble bath, going under water and provoking a wave that would flood the bathroom, is the theater of memory. As they burst, the bubbles reveal the past in all its playfulness and pain.

Today, these bubbles lead me to the beachcombing we practiced in Beirut during the war, and to 1985, the year of the jellyfish.

We had never seen jellyfish before, or perhaps it was only I who didn't remember seeing them. When they came, they contaminated the water by spreading their tentacles like an aquatic minefield. These creatures, which people attributed to pollution, were messengers of great calamity. It was as if the gods had sent them to punish us for our hubris, our affront to war, our denial of the *real* pain of others.

The jellyfish arose from below, from afar, joining the carnival of war. The barbarians, for whom the Romans longed as they partied on the hills of their eternal city, had finally appeared in the shape of sea creatures that would sting and awaken us forever. It was our day of reckoning.

That summer, Lebanon was consumed by the War of the Camps (*harb al-mukhayamat*), which pitted Lebanese militias loyal to the Baathist regime in Syria against Yasser Arafat's Palestinian fighters and their Lebanese supporters. Beirutis thought that Arafat and his fighters were wealthy, flush with petrodollars pouring in from the Gulf States. It was said that as militiamen were besieging the camps and firing at its inhabitants, Palestinian fighters would hurl Cadbury chocolate bars and exotic fruits at them for respite. These were the anecdotes from the War of the Camps, jokes and rumors that veiled the spectacle of slaughter inside.

That year, school closed early, extending our beach season. Only the boldest were at the beach: my family and a few others, a couple of dozen children and adults, going about their daily combing. As I was swimming in the *crique*, I started hearing whistling bullets fly over our heads. The camps were not far, a couple of miles away, but far enough for Beirutis who had mastered the art of compartmentalization and dissociation. The other children and I tried to continue as usual until we saw someone pointing from the restaurant overlooking the beach. Yelling and pointing! Yelling and pointing! He was pointing at a man lying in the sun close to where my parents and their friends used to sit. In the commotion, people started running, not knowing what had just happened.

It was Ahmad. He had been shot in the head.

Ahmad was the son of close family friends, the eldest of three boys and a girl. In his early twenties, he was tall and handsome, a courageous swimmer and an avid beachcomber. He worked on his tan and on his butterfly strokes all summer long. The bullet, nestled in the back of his head, caused him to go into a coma and then into a vegetative state, only to die some ten years later. I visited Ahmad in the hospital in Beirut

and then in London. I had to wear gloves and a mask
to enter his room.

They never extracted the bullet from his head.
They couldn't. The bullet became part of his being.
His gray matter wrapped itself around it, cradling it
like a lost child that had finally found refuge from
war. Ahmad cradled this foreign object, holding on to
it as if holding on to life itself.

The beachcombing we all practiced could not keep
war away or remove its offspring from Ahmad's head.
War had finally come to us and forced us to embrace
it on its own terms.

That year, 1985, put an end to our combing rituals,
our daily inventions of reality at the edge of the city.
The illusion of cohabiting with war in this carefree
enclave had finally been shattered. That summer, my
sister married and left home; the woman who raised
me and who had been living in our house for fifteen
years left as well; the Lebanese pound was devalued
overnight, squandering whatever was left of my parents' savings; and my brothers went abroad after graduating from college.

Nineteen eighty-five inaugurated my adulthood at
the age of twelve.

The bullet that put Ahmad to sleep awakened us
all from our dream in the sun. We knew we could no

longer swim, fish, and play *palettes*. War had finally caught up with our game at the beach.

Ahmad's bullet lives in my head. Its burning metal prevents me from forgetting or taking the currents and tides for granted. The hole in his head became my portal to a life I suffered, loved, and lost. I can't say I was traumatized by war; perhaps I don't allow myself this experience. I have accepted the fact that the bullet cannot be removed, that it's there, alive in me as I hold on to it in my own way. It became a point of entry and exit through which memories come and go like air, water, and waste. I can't pour concrete on it as Beirutis usually do.

Through ebbs and flows, the memory that comes from afar, swimming toward me, is embodied in writing. Its movement mimics that of water, going in and out of the *crique*, which controls the flow of the waves and the bodies jumping to catch them. As the waves crash on the rocks, they reveal the valuable, the painful, the bruised bodies of bold swimmers, and the aging beachcombers finally embracing their vulnerability.

Like the war scars that mark a few remaining buildings in Beirut, Ahmad's bullet scars me and allows me to remember and to forget my childhood, my life in war.

3

SEDIMENTS

My mom lines up her bottles of water on the kitchen counter like a regiment of soldiers. There are a dozen or so of them that she fills up from her drinking-water faucet. She then stores some more in the fridge in case some guests ask to drink it cold.

"You never know," she says, "when we might run out of water."

The civil war gradually eroded Lebanon's infrastructure. No pipe system was left untouched, neither that for drinking water nor that for what we call "service" water, used for washing and cleaning. With little chlorination to kill germs and bacteria and no filtration, the water that flows through these old and rusty pipes contains high levels of salts, lead, and other impurities. This forces everybody to buy water—except for my mom. She still drinks tap water, which gives her a special immunity and a mysterious glow.

My mom stores water and food items as if she were still living in a time of war, anticipating penury and closures at any moment. She is oblivious to the passing of time and expiration dates. When I stay with her during the breaks, it takes me a day or two to realize that the food or sweets lying around could be a day or a month or even a year old.

Furnished during the late seventies in an eclectic, baroque style, my mom's apartment is a veritable war museum. In this museum you find silk sofas, brass chandeliers, Persian rugs, crystal bonbonnières, and hundreds of knickknacks strewn across tables and shelves. These objects, which require an army to clean, are witnesses to a bygone era. As the dust settles on and around them, they await those who have left yet might return one day: a dead husband and children who now live abroad. But until then, nothing can be touched, and especially not my mom's water bottles. She is unfazed by cleanliness arguments and hoarding accusations, no matter how convincing or scientific they might sound. She has her system and knows where everything is and should be, until she decides otherwise.

But what system lets water sit in bottles for weeks and months? One can see in the bottoms brownish sedimentation, a mix of mud with yet-undiscovered particles.

———

The first thing my mom drinks in the morning is two cups of warm water. She warms the water either in a pot on the stove or in a little electric kettle, depending on the availability of electricity that day. She tells everyone that drinking warm water in the morning flushes out all fats and poisons and ensures a vigorous metabolism and a radiant, milky skin. For a woman who was born during World War II and who abhors needles and knives, water holds the secret to her beauty. It accentuates her big blue eyes and earns her compliments wherever she goes.

My mom's recipe for healthy living can be traced to a series of books on homeopathic medicine by Sabri Qabbani, a doctor from Damascus who belongs to the Syrian branch of my mom's family—the Qabbanis (or Kabbanis). He started a radio show and a magazine in the fifties that advocated healthy eating habits and lifestyles. His work became a bible for the generation of enlightened Arabs who came of age in the second part of the twentieth century. Having survived wars and famines, colonialism and nationalism, this generation would focus on physical health and stress reduction. Unknowingly, perhaps, they were getting ready to confront far greater horrors that lay ahead.

Qabbani's book *Your Doctor by Your Side* occupies a special place in my maternal grandfather's library. Entire paragraphs are underlined and copious notes are found in the margins. The book includes detailed advice on nutrition and disease prevention, and recommendations on how to avoid depression and bad moods.

In the chapter "Laugh...Laugh...You Will Heal," Qabbani describes the reaction of the nervous system to sadness and stress, the poisons of the modern age. He explains how adrenaline is secreted and by which gland and to what effect. Ultimately, he advances a radical thesis: "To preserve mental and physical health, avoid depressing places, never attend funerals, and never—ever—read sad stories."

In addition to following Qabbani's eating and drinking regimen, my mom embraced his "no sadness, no badness" motto. Her father, uncles, and aunts lived long and healthy lives, well into their nineties. Good genes, coupled with Qabbani's recipes, have given my mom special pride in belonging to a family that has managed to reap the benefits of modern life while keeping its poisons at bay. And she would never allow anything or anyone to come in the way of her healthy rituals and family pride. No doctor could ever take the place of Sabri Qabbani in my mother's heart.

But fate had other plans—most notably, my father.

After my mom married a gynecologist in 1970, her homeopathic worldview came crashing into that of Western medicine. My dad suffered from ulcers and heart disease and was a heavy smoker and prone to stress. In the face of this, my mom defended her eating

and drinking rituals and good mood with great feroc-
ity. And when she gave birth to her only child, she
had a natural birth and decided to breastfeed. It was
only when the ungrateful four-day-old bit the nipple
that fed him that she decided to wean him, unmirac-
ulously transforming milk to formula.
The weaning episode, which I heard about repeatedly while growing up, caused Mommy a great deal
of sadness. With time, I understood that the *infanta
dentata* out to bite and hurt had to be stopped so
that mom's recipe for healthy living could continue
undisturbed.

While my mom gave her little cherub formula to
preserve her milky skin, Hagar from the Bible gave
her son Ishmael water so he could survive in the desert and found a nation. Unable to bear children to
Abraham, Sarah offered her handmaiden Hagar as a
mating partner for her husband. But soon after Hagar
gave birth, Sarah miraculously got pregnant. With the
worsening drama between the two women and their
boys in the household, Sarah asked Abraham to repu-
diate Hagar and her son.
The exact details of the story vary across monotheistic traditions and texts, from the Midrash to the
Bible to the Quran. In the Muslim version, Hagar and
her son found themselves in an arid wilderness, forcing the poor mother to run seven times between two

hills in a desperate quest for water. Exhausted and on the verge of giving up,

> *She saw an angel at the place of Zamzam, digging the earth with his heel (or his wing), till water flowed from that place. She started to make something like a basin around it, using her hand in this way, and started filling her waterskin with water with her hands, and the water was flowing out after she had scooped some of it.*

Hagar saved her son by running back and forth between two hills. In doing so, it was as if she had activated a pulley, working horizontally to get the water up to the surface to be stored and then consumed. In memory of this, Muslims during their pilgrimage to Mecca reenact Hagar's quest between the two hills, which is complemented by the vertical movement of water. The angel Gabriel descended like a giant eagle, battering the earth with his powerful heel to bring water up to the surface. This bird of heaven dug a well as people do today, by piercing through the layers of earth to release the liquid of life. Water thus came from above and from below, delivering Hagar and her son from the wilderness and fulfilling what was written in the stars.

The story of water and the interchangeability of water, milk, and wine have been staples of Middle

Eastern beliefs and culture since before the wedding in Cana. From Jochebed's tossing of her son Moses in the Nile only to see him return as a prophet, to the Zamzam Spring spurting out of the warm sands near Mecca to keep Hagar and her son alive, water is at the origin of mother-son relationships and of monotheistic religions at the same time.

In the region's mythologies, water is best represented by the constellation Aquarius—the Water Bearer, controlling flows, temperaments, and destinies. His name is associated with the Latin word for water, *aqua*, which has Sanskrit roots. Aquarius carries a large jug and pours the water from high above, causing rivers to overflow and human destinies to tumble. As it gradually makes its way to the ground, water creates pathways that take the shape of the scars that one carries, and of the lines of one's palm. The water is poured slowly, gently, leading heroes to falter as they embark on their journey. Consulting the stars or reading palms is a way to decipher whether the hero will live or die, whether a mother will go on a maddening quest for water to save her son or whether she will walk into the horizon while he cries at the sky.

Some Greek sources reveal that the constellation Aquarius is based on the story of a beautiful Trojan prince named Ganymede. It is said that Zeus himself abducted this young prince so he could refill his cup with nectar on Mount Olympus. In the *Iliad*, Homer tells us that Ganymede was "the most beautiful of youths, so much so the immortals raised him up on high to be Zeus' cupbearer and live with them." When Zeus saw Ganymede playing on the hills of Troy, he was unable to resist his beauty. So he disguised himself as an eagle and swooped down from high above to grab the young prince. It is said that seeing him being taken away, Ganymede's dogs kept barking at the sky.

Water is at the origin of miracles, myth, and love of all kinds. In fact, much of Arabic and Persian love poetry is dedicated to the figure of the beautiful cupbearer or waiter known as *al-saqi*, who initially started pouring water and then quickly moved to wine. With every pour and every glimpse of his beautiful eyes, the cupbearer makes time flow.

Avenzoar (Ibn Zuhr), a twelfth-century Andalusian physician and poet from Sevilla, composed one of the most iconic poems about the cupbearer, which has made its way to us in song:

> *O cupbearer, our complaints are addressed to you;*
> *We have called upon you even though you do not*
> *   listen!*
> *Many a drinking partner have I loved for his bright*
> *   face,*
> *And from his hands have I drunk wine!*
> *Whenever he was aroused from his drunkenness*
> *He drew the wineskin toward him, sat back on his*
> *   heels,*
> *And gave me to drink four [drinks] from four [cups].*

What is wrong with my eye that it is blinded by a
glance?

The cupbearer is the handsome lover, the savior, and the decider of fate up in the firmament. The poet calls on him to hear his complaint, refill his cup, and fulfill his destiny. The cupbearer can relieve the poet from his worries by listening and pouring more wine. Through his beauty and attention, the cupbearer allows the poet to dream and to gaze at the stars that reflect like a mirror his past and future.

Life's mystery, which starts with water, leads to different pathways and desires. It leads explorers and poets to seek out water's origins, following rivers like the Nile upstream, or excavating the site of Ganymede's abduction on the hills of Troy, in modern-day Turkey. In this part of the world, where all life starts with water, fountains and creeks and songs about cupbearers arouse the imagination and connect people to ancient recipes and secret writings. When visiting the Middle East in the 1840s, the French author Gérard de Nerval described the water boutiques of Constantinople, marveling at the bottles' various provenances and properties:

> *In shops of this sort, you can buy the waters of*
> *different countries and different years. The Nile*
> *water is the most esteemed: it is the only water that*
> *the Sultan drinks, and is a part of the tribute paid*

*to him from Alexandria. It is considered favorable
to fecundity. The water of the Euphrates, somewhat
bitter and a little sharp to the taste, is recommended
to the weak and debilitated. Danube water,
strong in salts, is favored by those of an energetic
temperament. Then there are waters of different
years. The Nile water of 1833 is highly appreciated:
it is very expensive and sold in bottles corked and
sealed.*

Nerval continues that for Europeans, water lacks
these homeopathic characteristics and holy origins,
which elevates it in the eyes of the Ottomans to the
status of luxury goods with distinct denominations
and production years that rival those of wine. For
Nerval, bottles stand on the shelves like sacred objects
that heal those who believe in their magic powers.
But to heal and nourish, water must first rest after
its long journey across rivers and seas. Perhaps this is
where Sabri Qabbani and my mom, descendants of
those sophisticated Ottomans, get their water recipes
and drinking rituals.

Years of conflict in the Middle East—and conflict
over resources, including water—made people forget
water's divine origin and miraculous properties. A
far cry from the boutiques of Constantinople or the
cupbearing on Mount Olympus or in Andalusia, the

water we drank during the Lebanese Civil War came in plastic containers. This water had no time for aging and sedimentation, no time to reveal the messages that came from the past and from high above. The war left no time for things to settle, or for reading and storytelling.

The iconic water container during the civil war was made of plastic and called a *galon* (plural, *galonet*). This Arabized "gallon," which broke with its Anglo-Saxon origin as a unit of measurement, circulated in Beirut in different shapes and colors. Some *galonet* were rectangular and had handles like suitcases, which made them easy to carry. Others were oval shaped, resembling the jar that Aquarius holds up in the sky. But the most common *galon* held twenty liters, about five gallons, and is the plastic version of the green metal jerrican used to store gasoline that was popularized by the American army during World War II.

In the building where we lived, every household had several *galonet*. Ours were turquoise and had red caps and held twenty-five liters of water. When they were empty, we stored them in the attic, and when they were filled, we lined them up on the kitchen balcony or in a bathroom. They were easy to distinguish from the neighbors' containers. Our *galonet* were unique, as they had been purchased long ago, even before the war had started. And they were large, which meant that there were people in our household strong enough to carry them, or obstinate enough to drag them up the stairs

until they reached their destination. It didn't matter
that carrying heavy things made one short, as I often
heard. I was determined to deliver the water to those
who needed it, including my family.

   With the electricity off for months at a time, we
had to buy water and find ways to distribute it to
every floor of our eight-story building. These were
the eighties in Beirut, a time of war and penury,
marked by bombings and interminable sieges. In this
environment, water distribution developed into an
elaborate economy made up of containers of different kinds, and of schedules and needs based on family
sizes and levels of cleanliness. As containers circulated
up and down our building, we became familiar with
those that belonged to the different neighbors. Water
usage revealed how often people washed or cleaned—
intimate habits being paraded for all to see. Containers' numbers, sizes, and delivery frequency thus
made for good gossip, exposing obsessive-compulsive
behavior (*sirseb*) and the gradual toll war was taking on
individuals, families, and apartment buildings.

   To fill the containers in our building, we had
to buy water from tanks transported by trucks. The
trucks would pull into our parking lot and empty
their cargo into a large metal cistern equipped with a
faucet for water distribution. And though we lived in
a modern building with a German-made elevator and
porcelain sinks, bathtubs, and bidets, the absence of
electricity and the sporadic water that came from the

water company into our pipes forced us to buy water
so we could bathe, clean, and drink.

It was the age of Aquarius. At ten, I was responsible for water distribution in
our building. I'm not quite sure how I got this posi-
tion, but I know that I was drawn to water like an
amphibian. To this day, the very sight of water brings
joy to my heart. Whenever the doorman decided to
wash the stairs, I would volunteer to help, hoping to
partake in the splashing and soaping that started on
the eighth floor and cascaded down the marble staircase to the building's entrance. Whenever a friend
came over, I would beg to have the red inflatable pool
on the balcony filled up so we could play and splash.
Water, due to its scarcity perhaps, was the language
of play and love, and the container of early memories
and lasting desire.

When the neighbors brought down their *galonet*
to be filled from the tank in the parking lot, I lined
them up and filled them in the order in which they
arrived. Once filled, the containers would be tied to
a rope attached to a pulley that we had installed on
the roof. The other kids and I would pull this rope
to bring up the containers to their specific floors: the
blue one to the fourth floor, the red one to the sixth,
and so on. It was a very simple system, one that had to
adapt modern living to a time that preceded electricity and running water, bypassing the faucets and pipes
that the war had now rendered obsolete.

Cupbearing was back in force, reversing the transformation of water into wine in myth and poetry and
undoing miracles at weddings near and far.

While the lack of electricity necessary to bring
water up to the different floors made us buy water,
the lack of water from the water company forced us to
dig wells and draw on groundwater. The day our well
was dug, I stood in front of our building watching a
gigantic drill pound the earth. The drilling was akin
to medieval warfare, with the ram crashing against
the gate of a doomed city. As the pounding went on,
first came a reddish mud, then a tanned viscous liquid,
and finally, finally, water, flooding the street and making the access to our building impossible. The diggers
laid a border of cinder blocks around the drilling spot
to control the overflow. But to no avail. The fluids
oozing out of the belly of the earth were engulfing
everything. I was bewildered at the transformation of
muddy fluids into a clear liquid that made its way to
the top and flushed everything out. It's as if I were
witnessing the drama of extraction, like a scene from
Genesis. The appearance of water at the end marked
the culmination of Noah's flood, but we did not know
if we had survived or drowned at the end.

Bombing cities "back into the Stone Age," as the
war hawks say, brought Beirut's ancient rubble back
to the surface. It forced one of the most modern cities

in the Middle East to face its long history of suffering, stretching from Job's lamentations on the Beirut coast to earthquakes, invasions, displacement, and
civil wars. This war forced city dwellers to dig wells,
buy water, and store it in parking lots and in makeshift
tanks in their homes. Every household had to install
at least one water tank in the attic, in the kitchen, or
even on the balcony. Well drilling, water distribution,
and tank construction and installation turned into a
prosperous economy, pushing inhabitants to renounce
in their daily chores, habits, and beliefs their modern
outlooks. This economy revealed desperate attempts
to survive the war and regain control over livelihood,
hygiene, and body functions.

The water we dug up and drank during the war
prevented us from forgetting the chain of being and its
volatile order, which could spiral out of control at any
moment. We assumed we were modern, but living our
modernity on the edge, as it was constantly threatened
by the portals and faucets through which gush the miraculous and the archaic. Obsessive-compulsive behaviors
to which the war had given rise or accentuated—and
which will only get worse with age, believe me—
ushered in a new archaeology of water. Digging deeper
in this site uncovers graves and wounds affecting stone
and flesh, cities and people, and mothers who eventually
let go of their sons to save their lives.

The war pushed Beirut to fit the perception of a
water-starved and desertic Middle East and to reckon

with its own geology, history, and name. In ancient Semitic languages, Beeroth (Berytus in Latin) means "well," which is also the origin of the word *bir* ("well") in Arabic. Beirut went back in time, traveled upstream to its genealogical origins, and reenacted its moment of creation for all to see. The city regressed, but sought out pathways that connected it to its past, and to its fate as prescribed by star constellations and the whims of youths pouring nectar in the heavens or filling plastic containers in parking lots. The wells that were dug up were real and mythical, saving people's lives and connecting Beirut to epics and tales from sacred texts. And just like in Hagar's case, the divine intervention during the war came in the shape of giant drills that broke with their hooves the layers of earth to extract water and save Ishmael's descendants from thirst and death.

The water immersion and distribution that I practiced as a kid during the war prepared me for the cupbearing I would practice many years later as a host at parties and dinners in times of crises. Beirut's famous "I love life" slogan, which shields its inhabitants from trauma and pain, swaps water for wine and enacts the miracle of survival in both dark and happy moments. But every time I return to my mother's house and contemplate the water bottles on her kitchen counter, I remember what we have lived through, what I'm not allowed to forget.

My mom stores her water bottles like a weight from the past. The water comes from pipes and faucets that keep the time of war flowing. The sediments in the bottom of her bottles are suspended like memories that refuse to let go of her, and her of them. The mud at the bottom transforms her bottles into crystal balls, flickering a past that awaits those who can decipher it. To do so one has to read the inscriptions in the mud, and to look up at the stars, gazing at the Aquarius constellation and the beautiful Ganymede in the hope of knowing whether the hero has survived or not.

To this day, my mom hasn't given up on her holistic system. She doesn't really drink from the tap because her bottles filter themselves—by letting the water sit for days on end, she has invented an ingenious system for purifying the impure. This ability to flush out the poisonous by leaving it undisturbed is the survival tool that she learned from her family and from Sabri Qabbani's books. Left to form sediments in the bottom of the bottles, my mom's water will not poison her but rather give her a special immunity, to go on glowing and smiling no matter the badness around her. This is how she survived the war.

My mom's system to filter both water and war is the same one that Nerval discovered in the boutiques of Constantinople—modern-day Istanbul, and my mom's favorite city. The sediments in the bottles are the sad stories that Qabbani warned against. They wait for me to read them every time I visit her. But as a Beiruti who grew up in the eighties and as a literary scholar who specializes in deciphering words in multiple languages, I find myself facing a text that I cannot fully understand. These are the dangerous writings that theories of literature warn against—those signs and words that take us down pipes leading to the origins of the self and of memory.

Those writings also lead us down the pathways of cupbearing during war, of caring for grown-ups who were drunk on conflict and beauty rituals. Do children feel cared for by seducing with cups and plastic containers those trapped in modern buildings with no elevator or running water?

The cupbearers of old Arabic poetry and Mount Olympus came knocking at the door once, carrying colorful containers of life in times of war.

4

A BOILING CAULDRON

Her name was Shafiqa (pronounced Shafi-ah). I see her stirring a large pot, a wooden spoon in one hand and a cigarette in the other. Occasionally she turns and drops a glance at me from the side of her left eye. Then she mutters some strange words that sound familiar but that I can't make out. Her words are gobbled up, as if spoken by people who died a long time ago.

Shafiqa is whispering over the large pot, pleading with the spirits of the departed to attend. With every rotation of her wooden spoon, with every puff of her cigarette, more and more spirits appear, mingling with the dish's ingredients. They rise with the billowing vapors, then dive back to the bottom of the pot to exhume the lost graves of a great hunger.

In her midseventies, Shafiqa had small black eyes and short brown hair that was evenly dyed. Her skin was leathery, and she had a mole above her right lip that must have been beautiful at one time. She was chill, almost blasé, as if she had seen it all. She said and did whatever was needed to get by: a little love here, a little pampering there, and even some drama when called for. She had a thick Beiruti accent. She amplified the *eh* and *oh* sounds and started every sentence with *wa-eh* ("oh you" or "hey you"), a vocative particle that drew attention to Shafiqa's mouth and lips as they opened wide.

She was a widow and lived by herself in Tariq al-Jdideh, a neighborhood on the outskirts of the city, adjacent to the Palestinian refugee camps of Sabra and Shatila. And though she had kids of her own who were married and lived nearby, she always loved to come and spend time at our house, especially during the month of Ramadan, where every night was feast and merriment despite the ongoing war.

Shafiqa came from Tariq al-Jdideh and from the past. Born in Beirut in the early 1900s, she was my father's maternal aunt. She belonged to a line of dashing women who overcame great calamities and embraced modernity with open arms. In my family house, there is a picture of Shafiqa and her sisters with their brothers, husbands, and children. They are posing in front of a waterfall in Mount Lebanon. The picture, taken during a Sunday outing sometime in the early forties, shows them wearing fashionable hats, shoes, and dresses. The men and kids hover in the background or squeeze to the side. And at the center of the photograph is Shafiqa's sister, my grandmother, standing tall with a radiant smile. She looks like the leader of her own small tribe, organizing outings and managing affairs of all kinds.

Shafiqa and her sisters came of age during World War I. They learned how to dress and love and cook against a backdrop of famine and genocide. During the Great War, the Ottoman army, which was fighting alongside Germany, requisitioned food and imposed martial law across the region. Compounded by a siege and bad crops, the war led to a horrific famine in Mount Lebanon. The famine, which rivaled in its magnitude Ireland's Great Hunger in the 1840s and 1850s, also affected coastal cities like Beirut. Survivors tell stories of dead bodies littering the streets. Despite their emaciation, the dead are described as having their bellies inflated, as if they had taken in all the air in one last gasp.

But unlike the Great Hunger and other catastrophes around the world, Lebanon's famine has no memorial or museum. We can only learn about this event from the food that Shafiqa and her generation made, the recipes that they managed to smuggle across the years. Their struggle for survival is captured by *Safar Barlik*, a musical film that tells the story of a group of villagers in Mount Lebanon trying to sneak flour to the local bakery under the nose of the Ottomans. Directed by Henry Barakat, with script and music written and composed by the famous Rahbani Brothers, the Lebanese Rodgers and Hammerstein, the film featured a large cast of actors, dancers, and singers—including the iconic singer Fairuz. World War I and its catastrophic famine are thus remembered in song and dance as a way to entertain the spirits that were now gathering over a large pot, communing with Shafiqa's breath and smoke.

Presiding over the stovetop, Shafiqa made old Beiruti dishes that came from the recipes of war and famine. She made *mbahtra* ("the pock-faced one," a frittata with potatoes and vegetables), *khabissa* ("the jumbled one," a Jell-O–like dessert with walnuts and pomegranate), and *mfattqa* ("the craved one" or "the ripped one"—a sweet pudding made with turmeric and tahini). In fact, no dish encapsulates the pain and wounds from the catastrophes of the past better than *mfattqa*. It was this dish that she was making on that day when a little boy came peeking through the kitchen door to watch her cast her spells.

Shafiqa rejoiced in how my dad would spoil and pamper her every time she came to stay at our house. For my dad, his last surviving aunt was "from the smell of his mother," to use the Beiruti expression. My dad loved to hug and smell Shafiqa—perhaps this is why in my family we love to smell each other as we hug and kiss. Every act of smelling is like inhaling the other person, holding their smell deep inside. And by smelling each other, we travel through time to recover a father's lap, a mother's embrace.

My dad's mother was called Khayrieh. I have one fleeting memory of her. I'm in her bedroom. She's sitting upright in bed; she must have been sick that day. I can't see her clearly, yet she is a presence in a richly textured room. I can still feel the weight of fabric every time I recollect the scene. There is a dark rug covering the floor, and velvet and other heavy textiles on the bed and against the windows. She must have been wearing a nightgown with a satin sheen. It was winter and she was receiving guests in bed.

Was this her deathbed? Did they bring me in to say goodbye?

Today, my mom offers the most definitive account of Khayrieh's demise. Once, a tall and stylish relative came to visit my grandmother. This beautiful woman in her early thirties was wearing a maxi skirt. These skirts were long and narrow, and reached all the way down to the ankle. They were made popular in the late sixties by designers like Oscar de la Renta and continued to be in fashion into the seventies and beyond. My grandmother saw the skirt and was instantly smitten. Khayrieh went shopping the next day and bought a maxi skirt. Despite being well into her seventies, Khayrieh was still coquettish.

But the first time she wore her new skirt, my grandmother tripped and broke her hip. The long and tight
skirt made it hard for her to walk, especially when she
had to maneuver around all the rugs and textiles that
enveloped her surroundings. A mere piece of fabric
turned into an instrument of death.

Khayrieh's broken hip never healed, and she died
within the year. The civil war in Lebanon had just
started. It was 1975.

My grandmother was a fashionista to the very end,
and a larger-than-life figure who left an impression on
everyone. People always loved her elegance and charisma, but never forgot her tyrannical streak, which
she exercised over her children and their wives and
mistresses. They frequently spoke of her humor and
wit as well; Khayrieh's company was coveted around
town, and she, it seemed, relished that attention. She
spoke her mind, telling jokes and using funny expressions that were almost dirty. Her audience always listened and cheered and asked for more.

She was friends with a family that had made its
fortune during the Great War, profiteering from the
sale of sugar, grain, and other ingredients used in old
Beiruti dishes like *mfattqa*. This family would invite
my grandmother to their mansion. And as her neck
was craned from admiring the gold-encrusted ceil-
ings, they envied her high spirits and good health.
They complained that they couldn't enjoy life anymore or eat to their heart's delight. They spoke of

ailments and diseases that made their fortune superfluous, tasteless.

There was some justice after all, and some schadenfreude on the part of those who went through hell and back to survive the Great War.

During World War I, my grandmother married an Ottoman officer when she was still a teenager. No one quite knows whether it was a great love story or a marriage of convenience. It is possible that when he was riding his horse underneath her window in the Assour neighborhood of old Beirut, she threw an apple at him. When he looked up, he was enamored. With Cupid's arrow in his heart, he could not bear living without her from that moment on.

Khayrieh had a daughter with her dashing officer and took the train to join him wherever he was stationed during the war. But the officer and the daughter got sick and died. What disease? Where were they buried? What were their names? She never said. It is as if that chapter of her life was erased, mentioned in passing, just like the calamities of war itself.

Following the death of her husband and daughter, Khayrieh returned to her parents' house in Beirut and prepared to marry again. My grandmother's second husband was my biological grandfather, so we know a few more things about him. We know that he was a tailor and suit maker in Souk Sayyour, a market in old Beirut specializing in men's fashion. There is a picture of him smoking a hookah while sitting on a chair outside his shop. He is staring at the camera with a powerful gaze. He is dressed in a modern suit and looks very stylish. He was, after all, from the Ariss family, which means "bridegroom" in Arabic, but also a handsome, sharp dresser, just like the groom on his wedding night. My dad and I look a lot like him.

My grandmother's second husband would die prematurely as well, from heart disease this time. The tailor of Souk Sayyour would leave Khayrieh with two boys, a third one on the way, and a reputation for being a black widow. But nothing could stop this Great War survivor: She would go on to marry yet again, also with an officer, who would be smitten in his turn and stay by her side until her last breath.

In 1930, my Muslim grandma from Beirut with three little boys married a Christian bachelor from the northern town of Amchit. It was one of the first interfaith marriages in Lebanon. But for a woman who survived World War I, crossing sectarian borders seemed far less perilous than crossing those of nations in times of war. At any rate, it seems that neither one of them had to convert. They got married in church and did a Muslim marriage contract as well. I'm unsure if that's even possible, but this is what I heard from the same trusted source—my mother—who managed to get all this information from Khayrieh in between gossip and fashion talk.

Khayrieh's third husband was called Joseph. He had thick white hair and an angelic face. It is said that he was her dead husband's friend and loyal customer, and that when he learned of his friend's death, he sought out his widow to present his condolences. The legend goes that Joseph fell in love with my dad first, who was just a toddler. He would put him on his lap, while my dad played with the officer's medals, grabbing at them as if choosing him for a father. Perhaps Khayrieh used my dad as bait in her seduction ploy. But whatever she had in mind, it worked. Joseph, the Christian from Amchit, married the Beiruti Muslim widow with three kids. And just like the one in the Bible, this Joseph would raise someone else's children.

My grandmother never had children with her third husband. She didn't want to. In fact, she told my mom that she had a few abortions along the way. What was she afraid of? That he would die as well like the two previous ones and leave her with more mouths to feed? My mom relates that Khayrieh was afraid that if she had children with Joseph, he might love them more than those from her previous marriage. No one knows for sure. Not even Khayrieh herself.

Joseph loved my dad and uncles as if they were his own. He offered them the best education, sending them to the Frères school and then to the Jesuit university in Beirut. The Muslim kids who kept their dead father's last name grew up learning the catechism and French. The death of their father and their mom's remarriage to a Christian officer disrupted social models and confused family lines. Instead of training as apprentices in their father's shop with a needle in one hand and thread in the other, the three little boys went into law and medicine, and grew up feeling that they owed everything to their mom and the saintly man with golden medals.

In return, Khayrieh demanded absolute obedience from her three boys. There are stories about how they used to bend down to kiss her hand in front of their wives and children as a sign of respect. They worshipped the ground upon which she walked—as the saying goes—that same ground that would be the site of her untimely fall due to a tight, long skirt. And following her death, every smell and every dish that reminded them of her became sacred, involving much ritual and great pain. So when Shafiqa came to stay over at our house, she came to bring her sister back into the world of the living. Like a medium, Shafiqa was calling on Khayrieh's spirit and that of other survivors of the Great War to appear over the stovetop, above that pot where a magic potion was brewing. Shafiqa's *mfattqa* stirred up her sister's painful journeys on trains in times of war, dealing with the death of children and husbands.

Shafiqa came to remind my dad and us all of this teenage girl who lived and fought and fell at the end.

My father was born fatherless. He pushed through those passageways and membranes and landed on the lap of a Christian officer with a chestful of medals. He became a gynecologist, a surgeon, and a great storyteller.

My dad's stories, which depend on mood, situation, and audience, are often heroic and involve convincing people to do things for him while using great charm. There was one about a trip abroad during which he convinced the manager of a fully booked hotel to give him and his stranded friends a room by speaking a language he barely knew. He also convinced a school principal to admit a kid below the legal age. Other stories involve lifting very heavy weights and winning many medals even shinier than those on his stepfather's chest. In fact, he was the world champion in weight lifting and there are pictures and trophies to prove it. What world? Is it the whole wide world or some university games or some other contest? No one is quite sure. But who cares about details; it's all about the stories and how my dad tells them.

Growing up with two older brothers who were close in age, my dad had to compete fiercely at school, in sports, and in charming others. And though the jury is out on who could lift more weight, it is indisputable that my dad won gold in the academic arena. It is said that he came in first or maybe second on the Lebanese baccalaureate, the dreaded exam that all high school students must take to enter college. Not only that, but he got it early, at the age of seventeen, and decided to take a year to study literature—or was it psychology?—at the Sorbonne before going on to medical school, first in Lebanon and then in the U.S.

My dad was learned and cultured. He loved to entertain and make people feel special. The charisma was coupled with an appreciation for the nicer things in life, including silk scarves and stylish clothes that could have been purchased in Paris or from Souk Sayyour. And though he was pretty much bald, he diligently applied emerald-green Yardley brilliantine on the few remaining hairs on the sides and the back. And then there are the colognes that he loved to pour on himself, especially Drakkar Noir by Guy Laroche. He even requested that upon his death, those preparing his body for burial should wash him with cologne rather than water.

Though he never knew his biological father, my dad learned how to sew as well, practicing mostly on round bellies and sometimes on little fingers. He had a sewing kit in his leather briefcase, always ready should the need arise. And just like his father, he, too, suffered from the crises of the heart at an early age. He had his first heart attack at forty-seven. I remember visiting him in the hospital. The room was bright and the mood joyful. He would survive this one and go on living for another ten years.

My dad lived a full life and went on to marry more than once. His first wife was an American woman whom he had met while doing his medical residency in the U.S. Things didn't work out and they got

divorced in the end. But he, too, would fancy himself
a widower, with three little kids for whom he had to
find a mom. And just like he seduced the officer with
golden medals to make him his father, the three little munchkins seduced their new mom by running to
her on their first encounter and calling out "Mama,
Mama." She cried and accepted his marriage proposal.

The similarities between my dad and his mother
don't stop there. After marrying my mom, he, too,
decided that he didn't want kids anymore. He, too,
was afraid that his new wife might love her kids more
than the ones he was bringing to the marriage. My
mom, who knew her mother-in-law's stories and
had studied her strategies meticulously, fought back.
Finally, I was allowed to grow and reach full term. In
fact, my birth became one of his top five "I saved the
day" stories that he told with great pride and panache
at dinner parties.

My mom's pregnancy was going fine. She went into
labor one evening, expecting a natural birth. Though
my father was an ob-gyn, he was not his wife's doctor.
He was in the operating room, nonetheless, observing
from the sides. But when the labor got prolonged and
I was refusing to get out—my mom always reminds
me: "You were about to kill me!"—my dad stepped
in, pushed the doctor aside, reached for the forceps,
and pulled me out. After not wanting kids with his
new wife, he finally redeemed himself and brought
little Tarek to life, saving mother and child.

But the drama doesn't stop here. After I was safely extracted from my heavenly tub, he *and* my mom fought over my name. She was called Elham (inspiration) and wanted to call me Elhami (my inspiration), simply to make me hers. But like the alert general who senses the enemy's every move, my dad acted quickly and said: "No, we will call him Tarek [the star, the striker], after Tarek ben Ziad."

Tarek ben Ziad was the Muslim Berber commander who conquered the Iberian Peninsula in AD 711. But what chance does military conquest stand in the face of divine inspiration—in the face of Elham? No matter the name, my mother would get her way.

Did I mention that I was born on December 25?

There is so much and not enough to say about my father, his exploits and his deep attachment to all his children. He loved to smell them just like he loved to smell his aunt, who used to come and cook for him to remind him of his mother, the survivor of the Great War. Perhaps he, too, could have not been born, lost somewhere along the way between Beirut and Adana, on one of those long train rides that his mom took during the war. But he was meant to survive so I could lose him as well, so I could retrace what this family has endured by deciphering smells and tastes and strange dishes with complicated names like *mfattqa*.

The dishes that Shafiqa made when she came to stay over ripped the present asunder to replay the great tragedies of the past.

———

Mfattqa (or *mfatt-ah*) is pronounced with a heavy *t* sound, dropping the original *q* and replacing it with a glottal hamza or *ah*. It takes hours to prepare and is almost extinct from home cooks' repertoire. It is made with rice, sugar, turmeric, tahini, and pine nuts. After soaking the rice, you first strain it and add it to boiling water, mixing in the turmeric, constantly stirring until the water evaporates. Then you add tahini, sugar, and pine nuts, stirring until the very end.

Making *mfattqa* is time consuming and requires great physical strength. The heavy pudding needs to be constantly stirred with a long wooden spoon to prevent it from sticking to the bottom of the pan. The stirring must continue until a chemical reaction takes place: the coagulation of the sesame oil contained in the tahini. This process of coagulation is called *fatq al-sarij* (ripping at the seam). Once it occurs, the dish is ready, and it's then transferred to plates to cool down.

Rooted in a process of ripping (*f-t-q*), the word *mfattqa* belongs to the register of fabrics and tailoring as well as medicine. The Arabic root *f-t-q* has given us the word *ftaq* ("hernia"), denoting a ripping at the seam of the body, within its membranes. It has also given us the word *tiftiq*, which means "craving." *Mfattqa* is thus about ripping and craving, about being ripped apart by one's own craving for something or someone, a lost parent or a lost generation that perished during a Great War and is almost forgotten.

In Beirut, *mfattqa* is traditionally consumed on Arbaat Ayoub (Wednesday of Job). On the last Wednesday of April, Beirutis flocked to the seacoast at Ramlet al-Baida to picnic, bathe, and eat *mfattqa*. Ramlet al-Baida is the only sandy beach on the otherwise rocky seacoast of Beirut. It's also the last public beach on the southern tip of the city. This strip of coast was a holy site for Beirutis—a place of communion centered on bathing and eating *mfattqa*. On this Wednesday in April, Beirutis head to the beach, singing and dancing to commemorate the pain and salvation of the prophet Job, who according to local legend had washed in the sea off Ramlet al-Baida.

It is said that Job washed seven times under seven waves in the Beirut Sea to heal from the scourges that God had inflicted on him to test his faith and patience. The inhabitants of old Beirut—the city with seven gates and seven founding families—wash seven times under seven waves and eat *mfattqa* to reenact Job's pain and salvation. Through its architecture, food, and rituals, Beirut, it would seem, is a city dedicated to the memory of Job, the most tortured prophet in the Bible, who was also a pious and prosperous man. All around him perished, including his plentiful flock and his obedient children. Even the skin on his body wasn't spared.

———

The people of the Eastern Mediterranean coast, stretching from Egypt to Turkey, all have a version of the Wednesday of Job. This spring ritual of healing and rebirth coincides with several other holidays, including Easter and Sham al-Nessim (Smelling the Breeze) in Egypt. The people of the coast all have their version of *mfattqa* as well. In Egypt, *mfattqa* is made with black honey, sesame, starch, pistachios, almonds, and black seed. The Egyptian *mfattqa* is recommended as a natural treatment for emaciation and malnutrition. This version points to a history of suffering in which the pudding serves as a restorer of health. But what caused the malnutrition and emaciation in the first place? Is it a great calamity coming from high above? Or is it something akin to the wars and famines that Shafiqa and Khayrieh endured?

Shafiqa came to make us stir the cauldron of *mfattqa*, initiating the family into a lost culinary art and a painful memory. We all realized that *mfattqa* wasn't just a simple dish or dessert, but rather an event, a craving, a ripping that we all needed to witness, a past we all needed to access by entering the kitchen and volunteering to stir the pot.

Mfattqa making reveals the trials of prophets and children, impossible births and rebirths, from my grandmother to my father to myself. It reminds us of those who died along the way, from disease and malnutrition, with no names or grave sites, and no *mfattqa* to bring them back to health and save their lives.

Beirutis forgot all about the famine and the Great War. They forgot that *mfattqa* could treat the emaciation of those who experienced the wrath of the heavens, from the time of Job to World War I and beyond. *Mfattqa* is made to nourish newborn children, fatherless children, and children who almost killed their moms but were extracted in extremis by a heroic ob-gyn and great storyteller.

Shafiqa came to call on the spirits of the departed to assemble over her big pot, rehearsing the trials of family and kin, transforming our kitchen into a stage for plays about motherhood, life, death. Shafiqa came to make us all stir the cauldron, to toil and labor and witness the miraculous scene of ripping, to retrieve forgotten pasts and great calamities.

What was the name of my grandmother's daughter? How did she die?

Shafiqa has died as well, and so has her cherished nephew, and almost no one makes *mfattqa* anymore. Instead, they buy it ready-made from Makari and Hashem in the Basta al-Tahta neighborhood, not knowing how it is made or what kitchen it comes from. All that has survived are hints and bits of stories left by the Great War survivors and their offspring. These stories are the ingredients of recipes for remembering and craving that allow a little boy who once peeked through a kitchen door one day during Ramadan to follow a path to the past, to find a way to the future.

5

THE FRENCH SUBMARINE

When I searched for the name Gérard Lavide, nothing came up. Nothing. I kept changing the spelling of his last name, taking out the *e*, adding an *s*, omitting the acute accent on the *e* in his first name, removing the quotations altogether...still nothing. No number of permutations yielded the desired record or old photograph that would prove that the principal of my French elementary school in Beirut during the civil war actually existed. I started thinking that the last name, *La-vide*, which means "the empty one," was in fact empty, a foil for another name that was hidden or withheld.

What if the *name* was wrong? What if it was not Lavide but something else? I wrote to my cousin and classmate to inquire, and indeed, she wrote back that it was either Lavit or Lavitt, throwing my search into

further disarray. Could it be that I didn't remember
his last name? Could it be that she didn't remember
it either?

Something about French spelling—about what is
heard and what remains silent, what is remembered
and what is forgotten—was at the heart of this as well.

The more I searched, the more anxious I became.
I started looking for other teachers and school staff
who were in Beirut at the time. I googled Madame
(Mme) Lavaine, who was my French teacher in second
grade (*cours élémentaire 1* or *dixième*). No luck. Again, I
changed the *a* to an *e*, "vain" to "vein." Still nothing.
I became convinced that these people who inhabited
the world of my childhood were fictional characters,
empty vessels that carried French culture and spread it
overseas (*outre-mer*) and then disappeared, like fireflies
that wither once their mission is accomplished. Or
perhaps our contemporary search engines don't access
the past, at least not to the past that I was trying to
recover by sifting fiction and memory. No matter. I
was determined to find my schoolteachers; some trace
of them must have survived in the digital ether, either
through a nephew or grandniece or because an old
student posted or commented on a class photo that
included them.

My relentless search led me to a digital archive,
Filae, which digs into French birth certificates and
other demographic records. Little by little, a few Lavides
and Lavaines appeared. Then I found another site,

Géopatronyme, which matched names with regions, showing many Lavaines in Normandy. It is very possible that Mme Lavaine, the redheaded giant who struck terror in the hearts of the seven-year-olds in her class, was the descendant of those Norse warriors like Eric the Red who also settled Greenland. Some of those same Vikings turned south, forcing the Frankish king in the tenth century to cede territory in exchange for protection from their own fellow raiders. Those same Normans (Norse-men) eventually launched an invasion that would change the face of England and the Mediterranean world. Their rule extended to Sicily and Jerusalem and beyond, pushing French culture overseas. Their expansion south and across time continued through their descendants like Mme Lavaine, perhaps, and her other colleagues who served at the Lycée Verdun, Mission Laïque Française.

Founded in 1902 by the French educator Pierre Deschamps, the Mission Laïque Française (MLF) was a vehicle for the spread of universal French values at the beginning of the twentieth century. *Laïque* means "secular" or "nondenominational," and it is often considered the grand achievement and greatest export of the French Republic. Teaching native children republican and secular principles, the mission sought to civilize them and turn them into French subjects overseas. It also sought to compete with the

Protestant and Catholic missionaries who were hard at work establishing schools in the region around the same time.

Building on earlier experiments in Madagascar, the first MLF school was founded in Thessaloniki, Greece, with Beirut coming second, thereby laying the foundation for a network of schools that counts today over a hundred establishments spread across the globe. Following in the footsteps of the Enlightenment philosopher Volney and other eighteenth-century secular preachers of progress, the founders and future agents of the MLF held an unshaken belief in their historical and educational mission. Upon his visit to the Middle East in the 1780s, Volney established the principles if not the spirit of overseas education in most unambiguous terms:

> *I will cross the seas to teach these admirable laws to the savage people—to distant nations; I will say unto them: Children of nature, how long will you walk in the paths of ignorance? How long will you mistake the true principles of morality and religion? Come and learn its lessons from nations truly pious and learned, in civilized countries.*

Volney's heirs at the MLF were equally determined to shine the light of French civilization and the Revolution by guiding the children of nature in the Middle East, Africa, and beyond so that they could walk the path of fraternity, equality, liberty, and, in my case, literature.

The light of French civilization and later colonialism was nowhere more resplendent than in Beirut. The mission's founders boasted that only a couple of years after opening their school in 1909, over 50 percent of the students were Muslim, a rate unheard-of in other missionary schools. Perhaps there is something about Beirutis that makes them particularly susceptible to French civilization. Perhaps they are unable to resist the beauty of the French language. No matter, the relation between France and Lebanon has always been special, warm, maternal, even. To many, France had given birth to modern Lebanon, to its borders and outlooks, even before the country became a French protectorate in 1920. To many more, France was also their country, and so was French culture and history and all its masterpieces of literature, from the plays of Racine to the novels of Alexandre Dumas. The discipline needed to forge republican subjects brought those native kids into French history and culture as legitimate claimants.

If freedom and equality are universal values that belong to all, then so should the provinces and rivers and forests from which these values emerged. "Give me France and French culture now!" I could say the same about Istanbul; I always felt that its culture was ours as well.

The more I searched for my teachers and school principal, the more distracted I became. I got lost in maps, dates, and colonial history. As the search portals led me to the Normans and their newly acquired lands in the tenth century, I started lamenting the decision to rename French regions after rivers, which I always found confusing. Geography was out of sync with History, I thought. Studying at the Lycée in Beirut, it was hard enough for us to have two different geography and two different history books, one in Arabic and one in French, one chanting the glories of Lebanon and its snow-capped mountains, the other those of France and Napoléon and the Sun King. Two worldviews containing their own delusions of grandeur intermingled and forged the imagination of a kid who just wanted to escape the reality of war and dream of castles and dungeons, princes and knights, and magnificent queens wearing rare diamonds and parures.

Did I mention that I ended up as a graduate student specializing in eighteenth-century France?

My school building was a beautiful castle painted in yellow that glittered in the sun like a golden temple. Located in Beirut's posh Verdun neighborhood, the school also had a basement level that looked like a dungeon and included storage rooms and the living quarters of the caretaker and his family. Hanna (John, in Arabic), his wife, and their children sold candy and other snacks to the kids at the break. The kids loved and respected them. But Hanna and his family were like strange creatures who rarely saw the light. Everyone knew that they must have committed some grave infraction to deserve this life in the shadows, behind the metal bars of their subterranean world. In a previous life, Hanna must have failed his French and math classes, and gotten behavior warnings (*avertissements de conduite*) for nonstop chitchatting (*bavardage*) and other disruptions. Hanna looked like a fictional character from a Dumas novel, a famous hunchback or a king of the court of miracles, tales we were reading in our French classes.

The message was clear: Hanna and his family's plight could be ours, at any moment, should we fall out of favor with a teacher by slacking off or not handing in our homework. I now think that the mere presence of Hanna and his family in the school's dungeon was a warning to all those who didn't give it their best (*peut mieux faire*), those who were average (*moyen*) or far worse, those who were just weak (*faible*). These were the notations with which teachers marked our grade reports during the class council (*conseil de classe*), filling the special comment sections with all kinds of judgments and diagnoses.

Class councils were held at the end of each trimester, bringing together all the teachers and the principal and even our sports coach to discuss every student's performance and hand in a verdict at the end. The councils were like revolutionary tribunals that tried and convicted those accused of sedition.

Today, they remind me of the promotion and tenure committees much feared in academia, and of the councils that Zeus held on Mount Olympus to determine whether the hero was going to live or die. Though the Mission Laïque was meant to imbue the values of the French Revolution and put an end to the savagery of the despotic Ottoman Empire and the Middle East more generally, it brought with it sadistic verdicts and shaming rituals that rival those public floggings and stonings that Western media loves to report on.

These were some of the honors and dishonors that the councils handed down at the end of each term: *Félicitations* (white cardboard, congratulations!), *Encouragement* (yellow cardboard, almost there!), *Tableau d'honneur* (blue cardboard, honor roll!), *Avertissement* (no cardboard, watch out!), and the ultimate, *Blâme* (you are in trouble!). I don't know anyone who ever got a *Blâme*, but I later learned that it was a French legal term, something that the Goncourt Brothers received for writing an inappropriate article in 1853. But no matter the verdict, we all had to bring the grade reports (*bulletins*) home and have them signed by our parents. There was no Family Educational Rights and Privacy Act in Beirut at the time. Some kids with bad grades forged their parents' signatures. Others tried to forge the handwritten official document itself, editing out incriminating evidence by using Tipp-Ex correction fluid and hacking score calculations. Sooner or later, they got caught, and the punishment was terrible.

When the grade report arrived in our household, it was either a cause of celebration and gift giving involving a stop at the Donald Duck toy store on the way home, or a cause for collapse and fainting, eighteenth-century style. When both grades and behavior were signaled out as concerning, threats of boarding school were uttered. Granted, this intensified when I started middle school and left the beautiful Lycée Verdun. The more dramatic threat, however, was to take me out of school altogether and force me to work as a waiter at a local greasy spoon, serving fava bean and chickpea dishes to nasty customers who abused the kids that worked there. Being slapped around every day at some dingy diner was the kind of Sisyphean plight that my dad relished conjuring up whenever he thought I needed a boost in biology or chemistry.

The worst report arrived when I was in seventh grade, during that awful year of 1985. I was barely twelve. I remember my dad telling me that he didn't trust me anymore, and that all his dreams for my success were dashed forever. I almost fainted. My dad acted like Muhammad Ali Pasha, the Egyptian ruler who used to receive the grade reports of the students he sent to Paris in the 1820s to acquire French enlightenment. The pasha wrote periodic letters to the students, admonishing them for constantly failing and disappointing him no matter how hard they tried. This is a topic I later explored in my research as I tried to understand a thing or two about education and power, and how Arabs became modern.

My father's disappointment with my sporadic bad grades was perhaps due to his heroic role in getting me into school in the first place. It was a year into the civil war when my mom finally convinced him to enroll me at the French school in Beirut. She had enough of me wreaking havoc at home and demanding everyone's attention, all the time, especially when a war was raging outside. The whole family had gone to the Lycée, including my brothers and sister and cousins, so it was expected that I would be admitted. The only problem was that I was too young. The French had a strict rule: kids had to be three or older by the beginning of the school year in September to start preschool (*petite section* or *maternelle*). I, on the other hand, would only turn three at the end of December, so no way would I be admitted. But my mother was relentless. Receiving his marching orders, my father rallied the troops and headed to the school to meet with the principal and get me in. He was ready for a showdown.

As he tells the story, my dad fixes his seating position as if in a yoga pose, becomes animated, starts gesturing with his hands, and acts away. Entertaining guests at soirées, my dad went on stage, reenacting events that now make up my historical record.

It was as if I was learning history by watching movies and live performances. This is how I learned how my dad went to meet my school principal—Monsieur Lavide's predecessor—to convince him to let me in. He explained to him the circumstances, emphasizing what a precocious little fellow I was, and how I was already speaking and maturing so rapidly because I was surrounded by older siblings and adults at home. My father argued, nicely but insistently, that the few months separating me from the age of three would not make any difference. I was also his son and thus could handle anything, especially all things French.

The principal, it seems, kept resisting my dad's arguments, invoking rules, some developmental psychology studies, politely rebuffing all of Dr. Ariss's points. When he had exhausted all his charm, my dad decided to execute the plan he had concocted all along. Interrupting the principal, he asked him if he could open the blinds so that he could enjoy the "nice view" that this sunny spring day was bringing. As the blinds were lifted, the principal discovered a military jeep parked outside the school, with a militiaman pointing a Soviet-made DShK machine gun at his office. He turned to my father and asked: "In what grade would you like me to admit Tarek?"

I started school too young, too short, but no matter; I had my brothers and sister there to defend me.

The war forced Beirut schools to reconfigure their admissions: some girl schools had to admit boys, some elementary schools expanded to take in upperclassmen, and so on. The differences between elementary and high schools and *lycées* and *collèges* stopped making sense during the war. These reconfigurations were due to the division of the city and the inability of certain kids to reach their schools, since they were now in enemy territory. So for a while, my elementary school had high schoolers, including my brothers and sister. I remember how my siblings accompanied me to class on my first day of school. I had some trepidations, but I didn't cry. My brothers came to see me at the break and gave me a sandwich. It was a good start overall, and in general, I was a good student.

But at the end of my second year, my French teacher Mme Yazbek wanted to hold me back a year. Married to a Lebanese doctor, she was tall, skinny, and had blue eyes. She was quite old and had graying red hair styled in a bun. She claimed that I wasn't mature enough for my grade, that I needed to develop more, and that holding me back would be for my own good.

My father was furious. He met with her and asked her to give me a test to determine my maturity level. Perhaps he wanted to spare me the fate of the *redoubleur*, the stigma to which the students who didn't do well during the year were subjected, separating them from their classmates forever.

I took the test. I was a little over four, but I distinctly remember that day. I knew I had a test that was going to determine whether I moved up a grade or not. I think the test involved a practicum and an oral part, recognizing shapes and colors and fitting them into the appropriate boxes, and answering questions Mme Yazbek had prepared. The test was administered at the end of the school day, when the other students had left or were in the process of leaving. I passed, it seemed, and my dad was so proud, so unbelievably proud that his little boy passed his entrance exam into kindergarten with flying colors—and cubes.

My family, like many others, took pride in French education, and this was especially true of my father Muslim by birth but having grown up with a Christian stepfather, my dad and his two brothers went to Collège des Frères de la Salle, and later to Université Saint-Joseph. French education, for my dad, and his brothers especially, was a way to confront the question of identity in a mixed household. The principles of the French Revolution and their promise of universality had practical benefits and local applications in a country like Lebanon, where its different communities jockeyed for power and privilege in a system shaped by regional and sectarian divisions.

My father loved French literature and could compose poems at the drop of a hat. French literature was a marker of feelings and sophistication, especially for someone who had spent a year at the Sorbonne before entering medical school. He also avidly read the magazine *Historia* and spy novels. He read in bed, in the afternoon, right before or after his daily nap. And while he read, I met with my tutor, Mme Dupont, who came every Monday, Wednesday, and Friday at four in the afternoon to help me with my homework and just speak to me in French.

Mme Dupont was in her early sixties. She had lived in Lebanon for most of her adult life, teaching at a school called La Sainte Famille and giving private lessons in French. Mme Dupont lived close to our house, in the Clemenceau neighborhood. She tutored the entire family before me, and now it was my turn, as the youngest, whom she had known since birth. My brother once told me that when I was a few months old, I peed on Mme Dupont while she was changing my diapers. It was an anti-colonial act, no doubt.

Mme Dupont had a son of her own, but he was in France somewhere, married with kids. And though she rarely saw him, she mentioned him often. She lived in Lebanon because she loved the sea and the food and the weather, and no war was going to make her leave. I remember her ring with an aquamarine stone, which she wore proudly, as if she were carrying the sea and the sky with her wherever she went. She also wore some lightly tinted prescription glasses that protected her from the sun—the body, after all, has its own needs, no matter where the heart of Mme Dupont lies. She also had a few friends and families who gave her roots and included her in their events, mostly the joyous ones.

Mme Dupont was part of our family as well. She came to my birthdays and got me gifts and could read my mind. She was the French granny I never had. I used to get home from school a little after three every day, and Mme Dupont arrived right at four, leaving me little time to eat and take a break. Gradually, I started to resent her and felt that I was getting too old for this strict regimen of Frenchness. I also began to realize that this elementary school teacher was unable to help me with the math and physics and biology assignments that truly caused me anxiety as a teen-ager. I was getting frustrated, and she felt it. She told me once: "I know that you prefer to be with your friends rather than be here with me." It hurt me to hear it from her, but we both knew it was true. The cord had to be cut. I told my mom, and it was decided to retire Mme Dupont. It was a transition from the blissful world of childhood to the awful teenage life and all its realizations, which I had to struggle with on my own.

But childhood was not always blissful, despite the sun-drenched memory of Lycée Verdun. There was horror and abuse there too, and they ran deep. The list of insults, like *bourricot* (donkey), *imbécile*, and *idiot*, that we heard every day, and the flying chalk and landing rulers ensured that we remained *sage*, courteous, and obedient no matter the chaos outside or at home. Every teacher had their own favorite punishment. And those we didn't experience, we heard of for sure. There was a teacher who threw pieces of chalk at the students, especially those who were all the way in the back, chitchatting while he explained some grammar rule. The chalks flew in the classroom, mimicking the sniping taking place outside. As for Mme Lavaine, she had a thin and long black ruler meant only for hitting.

Depending on the severity of the infraction, punishments included public beatings with rulers and sticks, on the palms or knuckles or buttocks, turning little Beiruti cherubs into eighteenth-century criminals like Damiens, who was tortured and executed in Paris's Place de Grève. The infractions varied from minor disruptions to first-degree crimes, including hiding the teacher's attendance sheet, gluing something to a desk or a chair, or some other prank of the sort. As we grew older, the sabotage evolved; the worst was sticking needles into the keyhole of our classroom's door during break so that the teacher couldn't open it and resume class. We were well into our teenage years then, and they had to call a locksmith and launch an investigation. They approached the matter as if it were the conspiracy that took out Julius Caesar in the Roman Senate.

The harshest punishment of all was not physical but one that entered our minds and shaped our fantasies. It was a simple sentence uttered by a teacher or a teacher's assistant that had become the ultimate threat and the worst nightmare: "We will dip your ears in yogurt and lock you up in the basement so that the rats can come and eat them."

One would expect to see this sentence engraved at the entrance of an ancient Egyptian tomb or a forgotten temple, like a spell meant to fend off looters. But no, not in Beirut and definitely not at our school. It was the oil that kept the wheel of discipline turning. And it wasn't just a threat or a mantra or motto like "In God We Trust" or the American University of Beirut's "That They May Have Life and Have It More Abundantly." The threat of luring and unleashing the rats on the misbehaving kids felt real, and at times it poked out its head and came close to our necks and ears.

I still remember the scene. I was barely six and I must have driven a teacher crazy. I was taken to a storage room in the basement and briefly left there by myself, awaiting the horrible punishment. Nothing happened, of course, and no yogurt was put on my ears, but I kept looking around, expecting the rats to appear at any moment. I can see myself today waiting for the rats. I see a profile of myself, with a background of old desks and beige walls. Although it was during the day, the ceiling lamp was on, because

the basement's small windows were quite high and
let in little light. The teacher's assistant led me to this
cell. I think her name was Julia, and she spoke funny.
Who knows, maybe she came up with this elaborate punishment threat herself. It was the late seventies anyway, Pasolini's *Salò* was out, and people were
undergoing all kinds of torture in other basements in
the city because of the war. Julia must have watched
Salò or read Freud or the Marquis de Sade.

The scene lives in my memory like a dream
awaiting interpretation. This is why, perhaps, I'm
revisiting the dungeons of Lycée Verdun, to uncover
something that has been covered up, a vessel buried in the foundations of my psyche, and of the ugly
concrete building that replaced our yellow castle that
glittered in the sun.

In Freud's case study about the "Rat Man," a
patient comes to see him to complain about obsessional
thoughts involving rats gnawing away at the rectum of
his father and fiancée. Freud diagnosed the patient as
suffering from obsessional neurosis. The Rat Man, who
would end up dying in World War I, internalized these
thoughts after hearing from a friend about a torture
technique practiced in Southeast Asia that consisted of
using rats to eat people's faces. Freud observed that the
Rat Man was also expressing anxiety about shameful
sexual acts during puberty, including masturbation.
These shameful acts are the ones that a father in Beirut in the mideighties would catch his teenage son

committing, late at night, and would make sure to tell him how betrayed and let down he felt.

Poorly lit rooms and colonial dungeons have a tendency to correspond, to make each other meaningful, becoming worthy of being remembered and stored in the unconscious like a perverse tale of discipline, education, and fatherly love.

Freud's Rat Man would eventually find his way to Orwell's *Nineteen Eighty-Four*, returning in the main character, Winston, who was threatened with having his face devoured by rats if he didn't betray his lover, Julia. He would also make it to Beirut, where another Julia would lead a little boy to a dungeon of fantasies, desires, and eventually, literature. The Rat Man also connects World War I to Southeast Asia, from the 1916 Franco-German battle of Verdun to the 1954 battle of Dien Bien Phu that marked the end of French colonialism in Indochina.

Did I mention that my school principal, M Lavide, whom I was googling to no avail, had served in Indochina and perhaps fought at Dien Bien Phu? He had brought back with him a new set of torture stories, to be played out this time in Beirut's elementary schools.

Through my torture threats and fears in that basement, a map of the self and of civil wars and colonial conquests and defeats was being revealed. To decipher it, I first have to lose myself in the map. Then, slowly, find my way through Orwell, Pasolini, and Freud, excavating family relations and the sequels of the Lebanese Civil War.

As I reconstruct the memory of M Lavide, piecing together this not-so-mysterious character, I imagine him fighting somewhere in Southeast Asia, paving the way for the Americans in what would be later called Vietnam. I imagine him in that scene from *Apocalypse Now*, posing as the bodyguard of the French family that Willard discovered in the jungle, carrying on despite the fall of their empire. I also imagine him with the French Foreign Legion, quelling some revolt in Africa, or working out on a beach in Djibouti in Claire Denis's film *Beau Travail*.

M Lavide was tall and fit and had a military crew cut and a silver tooth that shone in the Beirut sun. He had a round, flat face and a mole that had slipped from an eighteenth-century painting and stuck to the side of his right eye. He lived in a house on the school premises with a little garden and beautiful flowers. Some teachers used to take us into the garden to catch butterflies with a net, just as in George Brassens's song "La chasse aux papillons." M Lavide had a little dog as well, a white bichon or some similar breed that chased after the kids with great excitement. I think it belonged to his wife or girlfriend, who was tall and blonde and who used to tan in the garden, surrounded by kids and butterflies.

It was appropriate that my school had a French officer as its principal. Beirut was in the middle of a civil war, and the school was, after all, called Lycée Verdun, a reference to one of the worst battles of the Great War. World War I was a European civil war as well, with family members from royal households and peasant stock fighting each other. We see this in somber documentaries about the grandchildren of Queen Victoria, and in films such as François Ozon's *Frantz* or in the series *Les Alsaciens*. People who lived in the same village or region suddenly became enemies and fought each other at Verdun and elsewhere.

The battle of Verdun, which started in February 1916, took almost a year to end and claimed the lives of a million men. They died for Germany's imperial fantasies and for the glory of the *république*. They died so that French civilization could spread far and wide, trampling the bodies of its youths and those of its colonized people, mixing blood with yogurt in the dungeons of a school in Beirut.

During the civil war in Lebanon, militiamen roamed streets that were named after the generals of the Great War and their resounding victories: Verdun, Clemenceau, Weigand, Foch, and even Allenby. While old Beirut with its seven gates and seven families was a city dedicated to the trials of Job from the Old Testament, colonial Beirut, which had seen the defeat and collapse of the Ottoman Empire and the triumphant entrance of the Allies, became dedicated to the

European civil war and the trials of French soldiers at the battle of Verdun. In these streets and neighborhoods lived our teachers, some of whom were kidnapped or killed during the war, and some of whom ran the school, taught sporadically, and disappeared for weeks on end with no explanation.

It was clear that M Lavide was the caretaker of these great generals, who won bloody battles and bestowed their names upon our city. He was there to make sure that their battles were not fought in vain, and that the legacy of empire and French civilization survived no matter what. He was also there to enjoy the sun and the sky and the bounty of this generous land, which everyone coveted. My dad and my uncle and other parents regularly invited M Lavide and his wife to their homes, to their beach houses, and showed them around. There were gifts, too, for Christmas and, of course, for teachers' day. It was a genuine affection mixed with a pact of mutual understanding that upheld or attenuated Sykes-Picot, the Franco-British agreement that divided the Middle East after World War I.

My parents invited our French teachers to parties and showed them the hospitality that befit the service that they were rendering. We never thought of them as high-class aristocrats or hyperdemocratic subjects clamoring for freedom. In fact, they were not a particularly civilized bunch or the imperialists that postcolonial theory would make them out to be. Nor did they present the romantic ideal of the French that we had read about in books. They were real, with real (or fake) names and desires. They loved gifts, clothes, invitations, and Lebanese food. We felt sorry for them, saw them for the expats that they were, far away from home with no family connections, and living through the war in Lebanon. True, they threatened and hit us from time to time, but who didn't hit to discipline in the seventies and eighties?

The food and gifts we gave them were little invitations to treat us a bit kinder, to help us succeed in fitting those images that our parents had of us. It was a competitive system, and my parents did their best to get us ahead, no matter the collateral damage to our bodies and minds.

One evening, M Lavide called my dad at home. "Bonsoir, Gérard," I heard my father answer. They chatted briefly and my dad immediately started getting dressed. He called my brother and asked him to accompany him as he went out. M Lavide needed a ride with people he could trust and who could get him safely through the city's checkpoints. My father arrived at the school with my brother riding in the back. They picked up M Lavide, who asked them to drive down to a designated spot on the coast. Once there, M Lavide got out of the car, walked toward the water, and took out a flashlight. He started flashing it at the dark horizon.

The blinking light, like magic, lured not a mermaid or some demon from *The Arabian Nights* that had been stuck in a lamp for a thousand years. No, none of that. As M Lavide flashed his light, a French submarine appeared.

It was as if the unconscious of war, including ours and World War I and Dien Bien Phu, had finally resurfaced, showing its head on that shore in Beirut. From the light carried by the agents of the Mission Laïque Française in Lebanon to M Lavide's flashlight, the history lesson was now complete. This night excursion involving an ancient combatant and a Lebanese doctor and his son who lived to tell the story over and over became my real introduction to French history, and fiction as well.

What was uncovered was not only a submarine and M Lavide's true or fake identity, but rather that in this tale, reality and history cannot live without fiction. Yes, the light that flickered on that dark night explains why M Lavide was so often absent from school. It also explains why, till this day, I can't even find his name in any record, virtual or otherwise. Perhaps he was a figment of my father's imagination, a character that jumped off from one of his spy novels, forcing the poor principal to perform that role, just like he forced his predecessor to admit me to school at gunpoint—or so he said.

M Lavide, this vessel carrying French history and education and colonialism, became empty again once he dumped his baggage, once his light burnt out. He was ripe for the filling when we—my father, my brother, myself, and others—turned him into a fictional character that we wrote in multiple versions, bringing him back into the books we were reading.

Let no one mess with our fantasy about France and French culture, or we'll put yogurt on their ears and shove them in the basement. When he couldn't play the role of a count or a marquis, he was going to be a French spy, something out of the series *The Bureau*.

The story of M Lavide and the story about enrolling me at school expanded my father's repertoire of the tales that he performed at dinner parties. These tales put war back in the book, not that of history, for it's too controversial or too painful for us Lebanese, but in the book of fiction. Like those books in the Harry Potter series that uncover worlds that we could enter or exit, open and close in a gesture, fiction allowed us the freedom to permutate, to shift an *a* and an *e*, so something is revealed in writing, in this story that ends with a flashlight and a French submarine saying *coucou* (peekaboo)!

This story is also about a special kind of imagination, unique but not so unique to my family and to French education, which invests more in the elements of the story and its performance than in details and facts. Perhaps the only way we can talk about the war is when we can write it as a spy novel and insert ourselves into its pages. This literary sensitivity that I acquired turned me into a lover of thrillers, historical novels, and the French language. But for a long time, I had to lock up this lover inside me, threatening to put him in a dungeon with yogurt on his ears, just like my dad had to lock up his so he could be a successful doctor and a good family man. But no more.

My only regret is that my father is not alive—he would have loved *The Bureau*!

6

MINA, MINA

The phone rang in the middle of the night. My father answered.

I can still hear his voice, murmuring, acquiescing, arguing, and acquiescing again. He had two phones by the side of his bed. One was a gray rotary phone that rarely worked, while the other, which worked a bit more frequently, was a beige push-button phone that my dad had installed halfway through the war. He was, after all, a doctor, a gynecologist, and he had to be always reachable in case a baby decided to push through in the middle of the night.

At one point, we had the only working phone in the whole building. Neighbors would come knocking at our door, asking to use the phone to call loved ones during the conflict's worst episodes. They needed to tell them that they were still alive, they needed to hear themselves saying that they were still alive, that they would pull through. But that night was quiet. The call was coming from afar, far beyond the green line that separated the two Beiruts. It was coming from a place more painful than war can ever be. It was my sister calling from America. She wanted to come home.

After spending nine months with her mother, my sister couldn't take it anymore. She had to come back, no matter the war that had shut down Beirut's airport. No matter the pain of her reunion with her long-lost mother. No matter the agony of separation when she was abandoned as a child. She wanted to return, and my dad had to arrange it. So it was decided that my sister would fly to the nearby island of Cyprus, and my mom and I would go and meet her there. We had to cross from the western to the eastern part, where the port was now located, take a boat to Cyprus, and bring my sister home.

Crossing to the East during the war involved going through borders and checkpoints where people had been detained, beaten, killed. There were multiple crossing points along a dividing line where vegetation grew and wild beasts thrived. This line split Beirut at the beginning of the war in 1975 into eastern and western enclaves, one allegedly Christian, the other, Muslim. This split, this wound in the heart and geography of the city and the country, caused population transfers, as the neighborhoods were often mixed,

forcing those who lived on one side to move to the
other, as if emigrating to a different country.

After the war, a special government agency was
created to compensate those who were displaced and
turned into refugees in their own homeland. Some,
however, stayed behind. They refused to leave their
homes, their neighbors, their childhood memories.
They simply couldn't leave.

The crossing points included the port, the Ring
Bridge, the National Museum, and so on. There were
times when only one of these crossings was open or
safe enough for those who could get through. People risked their lives to cross, taunting whimsical and
sadistic snipers. At times people had to cross by foot
the no-man's-land and clear the checkpoints to get to
the other side. Business activities grew around these
crossings, with people selling food and beverages
while others offered taxi and bus rides.

Other crossings connected Lebanon's northern province to Mount Lebanon, which included
an infamous one by the sea called Barbara. That
crossing was the most feared, as it was believed that
Muslims, Palestinian refugees, and leftists of various
factions would be kidnapped and liquidated on the
spot if they dared to come close. The Barbara checkpoint was named after the coastal town where it was
located. Barbara also refers to the saint whose per-
secution by the Romans is commemorated by Eastern Christian sects at the beginning of December in

a ritual akin to Halloween. Her suffering is reenacted by the wearing of masks, other disguises, and making a sweet wheat pudding garnished with red pomegranate seeds.

I remember crossing the Barbara checkpoint as a kid. I was with my family, heading from the northern city of Tripoli to Beirut. I could still recall the terror I felt as we got close, wondering whether they were going to pull us over, interrogate us, make us disappear. The name Barbara has a special ring, carrying with it the residues of war, the economics of revenge, the afflictions of a Christian heroine, and the excitement of a ritual that unleashed wild desires, outrageous disguises, and deep anxieties.

The crossings redrew the map of Lebanon, disrupting our experience of time and limiting our freedom of movement. A twenty-mile journey could take hours due to circuitous routes invented just to avoid one checkpoint or the other, or due to long waits in the car as militiamen checked IDs and searched for bombs and enemies. Like a weather report in the Northeast U.S. during winter, a report on the crossings during Lebanon's war was the first thing that people checked in the morning. These weathervanes reflected a political situation whose pulse and vitals needed to be always monitored.

When the war ended in 1990, I met people who had never been outside of their own enclaves. Some friends in the East thought that West Beirut was like a jungle full of wild animals—though they were not the only ones who thought that—while some friends in the West thought crossing to East Beirut meant being detained and killed on the spot.

My father, who went to school in what had become East Beirut and had family and friends who lived there, insisted on crossing throughout the conflict. Once, he was detained. West Beirut was experiencing a severe gas shortage, so he decided to drive to the other side to fill his tank. He rode in his white Honda Prelude to the checkpoint. They pulled him over and started questioning him.

"Where are you going?"

"What is your sect?"

"What is your business?"

"Come with us!"

They told him that they were going to hold him hostage and exchange him for people from the East held by the other side. My dad joked and flirted with them, told them that he would love to be held hostage, that he would love to be plucked away from his routine and drudgeries in the West. But they should realize as well that this sophisticated Beiruti doctor would need a nicely furnished apartment and a well-equipped office so he can see patients in the East. They laughed. He laughed. They let him go. They liked him. Perhaps they were bored that day and weren't in the mood for war. Or perhaps they recognized his refusal to succumb to war's logic.

My dad's biggest achievement during the war was obtaining an army-issued ID stating that he treated patients at a military hospital and required safe passage. This meant that we found a way to go back and forth between East and West Beirut a little easier, a little safer, bypassing the interminable lines and transcending sectarian and factional divisions. This ID was a reward for his unwillingness to live by the rules of separation from his friends and family in the East. By crossing from West to East, and from the seacoast to the mountains, my dad managed to defy the geography of war.

I'm not sure why my dad didn't accompany us to Cyprus to go get my sister. Perhaps he was busy at work, waiting for one of his patients to give birth. No matter. My mom and I embarked on the journey by ourselves. I don't remember how we crossed that day, but we made it safely to the port, where we took a boat to the island, which is only 160 miles away.

The boat that took us to Cyprus was called *Aphrodite*. It had big blue and white stripes. I remember seeing families, first gathering on the deck and then gradually moving to cabins and common areas to rest and sleep during the six-hour journey. There was a kid my age or a little younger whom I saw playing on board, and whom I would later see sleeping on a couch, covered by one of his parents' coats. I still remember the look on his face, sleeping so innocently, as his family escaped Lebanon's war through one of the last remaining outlets—the port.

We arrived in the coastal city of Limassol in the afternoon. It had become a haven for many Lebanese, some of them moving there permanently and others, like us, visiting for an occasional respite. I still remember the amusement park with its pinball machines and bumper cars, and the coarse black sand of Limassol's beaches. Even as a child, I always thought that our beaches had richer colors and silkier textures. But there were other beaches in Cyprus that young adults flocked to and that were supposed to be nicer and more idyllic. I had heard about Ayia Napa, where, it was said, girls sunbathed topless. But that day we were not going to the beach. We were on a mission to bring my sister home.

After disembarking, my mom got us a taxi to the airport in Larnaca, where we waited for my sister to arrive. The experience of time for a child on such a journey is elastic at best. The wait might have been a few hours or one or two. I have a memory of the airport, perhaps a conveyor belt and a cart. All I remember is that my sister finally arrived, and we immediately got another taxi to head back to the port in Limassol, and from there on to Lebanon. Speaking mostly in English to the Cypriot driver, my mom uttered a word in Arabic to confirm our destination. She said, *mina*, and he repeated after her, *mina*. It was as if they were communicating in a secret language that only they could understand.

Mina is the word for port in Arabic. It's an ancient word that harkens back to the seafaring history of the region, and to the Ottoman and Mediterranean world that connected Cyprus to Lebanon and Greek to Arabic and other languages from the coast. The exchange of the word *mina* between my mom and the driver was like the utterance of a magic word that suddenly reconnected a landscape and a people that were torn apart by a century of wars.

The magic word *mina* was also bringing home an errant ship, the daughter that had flown all the way from America to reunite with her Eastern Mediterranean family. Aphrodite was coming home.

My sister had green eyes and long, curly hair. Her hair was light brown, and the summer rays accentuated its golden highlights. She had been born in Kentucky and was my dad and his American wife's firstborn, followed by two boys. She loved reading, windsurfing, seashells, pita bread, and cheese. She left Beirut when she was seventeen, only to return some nine months later looking almost unrecognizable to the little brother who missed and longed for her.

I remember distinctly noticing the change when we got into the cabin on the way back to Beirut. Her gestures were different. Something about her vivacity was gone. She was exhausted, no doubt, but it was more than that. America must have done this to her. She sat on the edge of the bed, opened her suitcase, and started taking out what she had acquired there. There was a bottle of cologne that she had gotten me as a gift: Jean Naté. With its French name, this cologne confused me as it was equivalent to another cologne with another French name that we had in Beirut, Bien-être.

Why did my sister go all the way to America to find Bien-être, which means "well-being" in French? On that bed, in the small cabin of a boat bringing back some stranded Lebanese so crazy as to return to the country of war, my sister was being revealed to me in a new light.

She had picked up knitting while living with her mom in Ohio. She brought back a yellow, blue, and white blanket she had made herself. All pastel colors. I remember the angles of this wool blanket: little peaks that went up and down, zigzagging like a mechanical heartbeat. This knitting was a form of writing with no words, invented by people in the cold corners of the world in search of warmth. Its movements went in and out and up and down to expand the surface of the blanket, to stretch time and extend the flat Midwestern landscape, to reach out to other people without uttering a word. It was a writing with little hope of communication, of connection, of intimacy. My sister was bringing back an impossible text, part travel narrative, part confinement notes, expressing what could never be expressed in letters or over the phone.

As I reflect on this scene, I begin to understand how I learned to read and decipher lines, curls, postures, and smells. I was beginning to understand, as a boy of six, that those who leave do not return as themselves, that perhaps some drastic alteration takes hold of them, changes their features, and makes their hair and skin colors fade away.

The scene lingers, as in a long shot that captures the curls of my sister's hair, the posture of her slightly bent body, and a sadness in the face that recalls Botticelli's painting *The Birth of Venus*.

In that cabin, my sister looked like a wounded soldier who had left the Lebanese Civil War to go fight in America. And like a true leftist and pan-Arab from West Beirut, she had gone to war against imperialism, engaging in an equally consuming conflict that pitted blood against blood. She looked tired, trying to cover up the shame of having withdrawn from the battlefield, of having given up on trying to reach the other side. There was also apprehension as she returned to reunite with those she had left behind.

The cabin we got on the way back from Cyprus had three beds. Mine was missing a pillow. When I exclaimed, "My bed has no pillow!" my sister immediately offered me hers.

———

It all started with another phone ring. This ring was coming from a past that no one wanted to confront. It was their mother. She wanted them to come to America. This mother, whom we all knew existed somewhere, in another dimension perhaps, had finally reappeared. She manifested herself through the phone that started ringing, calling my brothers and sister, awakening an ancient wound.

Their mom was calling, and she wanted them to come and live with her, to reclaim them after a decade of separation. Their mother was calling, and they had to make a choice, they had to take sides in a feud in which they were the victim, then, now, and forever.

The phone kept ringing for days, and no one could ignore it. Seen through the eyes of a child growing up with his loving brothers and sister—the only siblings he has—the house was becoming unrecognizable. The fights were no longer between my mom and dad about some inappropriate gesture or flirt at one of their parties. Nor were the fights playing out in the living room or in the kitchen for all to see either.

No one yelled anymore. It was a terrible silence, broken only by phone rings in the middle of the night, louder and more terrifying than the bombs and bullets of the civil war. The fights now went behind closed doors that kept shutting all the time, hiding an impossible secret, announcing a doom that would break my family forever.

Their mom was calling, and they had to choose. Now, a different war had entered our house and was threatening to make my siblings disappear.

The origins of this conflict started back when my dad went to the U.S. after graduating medical school in Lebanon. He was supposed to complete his training and obtain his board certification and come back and marry "the best girl in Beirut." These were the fifties in Lebanon. Few were those who went to the U.S. to study, let alone to study medicine. But my dad fell in love and married a beautiful woman, a nurse at the hospital where he worked. Years later, I saw a Hollywood movie set during that period about nurses and doctors falling in love that gave me a glimpse into that world that my father had inhabited.

After having two children in the U.S., my father and his wife returned to Lebanon, where they would have another boy. My dad describes the decision to return as an Arab nationalist one. He used to tell the story of how he refused American citizenship, how they called and begged him to take it, but he had categorically said no. He said no to America. What would a French-educated Lebanese and proud Arab do with American citizenship? He admired Egypt's president Gamal Abdel Nasser, a leader who filled the Arabs with pride and fantasy of a different kind. My dad was not going to abandon his identity to pursue the American dream.

Something about America must have disappointed him as well, and he, too, had to come back. But he was going to bring back his beautiful wife, who looked like the movie stars that filled him with wonder. He thought that he had found a way to have both Nasser and Hollywood in the end.

There is a whole genre in Arabic literature about men studying in the West and falling in love with women there. Eventually, they find themselves torn between their desire and love for these women and their duties and obligations to families, clans, homelands, and Arab causes. We see this struggle in the works of Tawfiq al-Hakim, Suheil Idriss, Tayeb Salih, Alaa Al Aswany, and others. These novelists portray the confused and disoriented Arab student becoming aware of his desire in Paris or London and later in the U.S., experiencing enchantment and disenchantment. Young men struggling with feelings of guilt of all kinds write letters of love and rejection, and mechanical letters that zigzag and reach no one, that get nowhere. In these novels, the European beloved is often called Jean, which is the equivalent of Laila in old Arabic poetry and song.

Love children, family breakups, and enduring unions are the varied outcomes of this narrative of desire, as important to understand as any cultural exchange or war between East and West. The pangs of love, guilt, and duty cut more deeply than the wounds of war. All this is to say that my dad was the product of his age, and as I reflect on his experience today, I remember the stories into which he was woven, knitted, and into which he tied himself. But my father thought that he could have it all, and maybe he could have succeeded. And maybe he did succeed a little bit, in some other ways, at the end.

When they moved back to Lebanon, my father and his small family lived in the same apartment building as his mother, in that place where he was born, close to the sea. Up an alleyway that was shaded by trees, his apartment got little sun, but it was right beneath that of his mom—where she reigned supreme over her clan. This matriarch who yielded incredible power over my dad and his brothers had now added a blonde American girl to her ever-expanding harem. And she wouldn't be the last one.

As the years passed, the fighting between my father and his wife intensified. It was the height of the Cold War. Lines were drawn. Then came separation, divorce, abandonment. I would later learn that their mother fought to take her children with her, but in a man's world and in Lebanon in the sixties this was impossible. She left. How? Why? In what state? She left. She had to leave. She must have given up. A year later my dad met my mom, asked her to marry him and become the stepmother for his three children.

When my brothers and sister left for the States, my father tried but failed to replace them with me, all that was left to him, coining a term that never felt real— "his dad's buddy" (*sahib abou*). After hiding his feelings for me for years in order not to make my siblings jealous, not to make them feel less loved because they had lost their mom, my father was trying to reconnect with me, but to no avail. His children, "for whom he sacrificed the world," as he used to say, had now left, and there was no replacement in sight.

In these feuds where powerful feelings of loss and betrayal arise, adults become children, making demands on their kids, requiring absolute loyalty, undying love, crushing them. My father was wounded, and all of us, myself included, had to attend to his wounds. The doctor was now the patient, and the father was now the child who understood but could not accept that his children would leave to reunite with their mother.

When I finally realized that my siblings were leaving, I started going into their room, trying to hide in their suitcases, under their desks, their beds, afraid that they would leave in the middle of the night, without saying goodbye, without me. But there was no room for this little brother's feelings. If anything, I was a mere spectator to a tragedy that had turned our house into a stage of gestures and whispers, phone rings in the middle of the night, ephemera that now lend themselves to telling the story.

My dad finally conceded. He started saying that he couldn't stop them from seeing their mom. He had to find ways to assuage the pain of letting them go after all these years of fighting to keep them. So he suppressed his feelings and bought them tickets, gave them money, and sent them off to retrieve this part of themselves that they thought had disappeared, that they were told had died.

I have no memory of their departure. No airport and no goodbyes. I realize that memory plays its own hide-and-seek, and perhaps this game is more complicated than we think. I had to wait till they started returning to learn how to read and recover what had been forgotten.

But as soon as they left Lebanon, my mom and dad decided to remodel our house, tearing down walls and building bookcases and installing carpet and wallpaper. It was an extreme makeover. Or perhaps it was like that scene from *Citizen Kane* when the old man had been abandoned by his youthful wife, who felt caged in. With no words to express his pain, he tore down her room, piece by piece, bit by bit. But my parents tore down to rebuild anew, to cover up the rubble inside. This is the Lebanese way, which often involves some kind of building or reconstruction project.

My mom, who had married my father and accepted being a stepmother to his children, whom she loved and cared for, was now going to reinvent the family as nuclear and biological. Perhaps this was her fantasy from the beginning—*her* husband, *her* child, *her* house. But the telephone wills it otherwise. While my brothers ended up spending two years in America, my sister, like the beautiful Venus or Aphrodite, decided that she had enough of confrontation on the other side of the world. It was time for her to stop trying to connect and return to her Eastern Mediterranean homeland. She eventually found ways to make it to port, *mina*, the portal that opens to a past with an uncanny familiarity and excruciating pain.

The blanket that my sister knitted and brought back from the U.S. recalls that of Penelope in the *Odyssey*. Penelope wove and unraveled, and wove and unraveled Laertes's shroud while waiting for Odysseus to return from the Trojan War. Except my sister turned the *Odyssey* on its head: she was both Odysseus and Penelope at the same time. Like Odysseus, she was trying to conquer a new world, reconnect with an old one, find her mother. And like Penelope, she knitted to preserve herself while away, protecting her bond to her father, brother, and city. The blanket was her security in dangerous lands near and far. Of all of us my sister is the one who lived the longest in Lebanon. She left again when she got married, but came back and settled there soon after, refusing to leave no matter how bad things got.

Knitting her blanket in the U.S. allowed my sister to keep home with her. But she also knitted her way back, she knitted a map that upends through its mechanical regularity the map of war-torn Lebanon, with its terrifying checkpoints, divided families, broken selves.

She was knitting herself together, holding herself up, surviving the cold.

In America my sister found a way to bear her displacement. Perhaps she knitted to find a common language with her new world, common threads and words that meet and recognize each other and cross over at the end like *mina, mina.* But no such words emerged, and the knitter had to move back to Lebanon, back to Beirut, where she would knit some more to reconnect with her old world, her old bedroom, which was now remodeled. Knitting for her offered a language and a geography that tried to defy silence, absence, and painful reunions.

Soon after her return, my mom got my sister yarn and asked her to knit more blankets for her room in Beirut. The blankets she knitted had bright colors with a lot of blues, like the Beirut Sea that she loved so much.

While the knitting allowed her to return, to find her way back through ports and portals, on planes and boats and across checkpoints, the Jean Naté cologne that she found there allowed her to re-create the smell of home. Perhaps it was the well-being (Bien-être) that she was craving, that she was trying to conjure up through the smell of the world that she had left behind. She was bringing them both back as testimonies of what she had endured.

Eventually my sister would find many moms, crossing the ocean back and forth to the U.S. and from West to East Beirut, repeatedly, for years to come. She even took me with her on these subsequent crossings. For a while I was her chaperone, "his sister's buddy," and that felt real and true. Perhaps she failed to redraw the map of the past, to cross and reconnect once and for all. But she succeeded in drawing the map of the future in those trials, through those constant peregrinations across borders and checkpoints.

There is no other side. There is no past to be retrieved, for it lives in us, in her. That's why the word border in Arabic (*hudud*) has the same root as the word wound (*had*). They mark the landscape and cut deep inside. They can never be overcome. We learn to live with them, crossing them over and over, soothing our entrails, calming that pain that comes from within, from afar.

7

MY SYRIAN MOTHER

I don't know what came over her that day. She grabbed my hand, took out the scissors, and started cutting. The sharp blades were gnawing at the line that connects the nail to the skin. Digging and cutting. Deeper and deeper. It's as if they were trying to erase a border that kept lovers apart for a thousand years. Perhaps she had seen my mother or my sister doing it and wanted to experiment on my little fingers. Perhaps she was angry and wanted to punish, hurt, cut.

I still feel her hand grabbing mine, suddenly, forcefully, carving my flesh. It was as if she had revived a ghoulish pain that came gushing through time in a frenzy, unable to hold its assault on my hands, on my body, on my memory.

When she eventually left our house, I took to the habit of cutting my cuticles. I had no scissors, and neither was I going to ask my mom for any, as this was what she and I had shared. I started cutting them regularly, methodically, as if I was trying to bring her back, to punish myself for having driven her away, to punish her for having abandoned me.

I used a box cutter and applied it to my dead skin. A few days later, half-moons would appear on the nails, marking the circular movement of the cutter. It was only in college that a friend noticed these half-moons and inquired about them. I felt exposed, embarrassed, as if something about my relationship to that woman was revealed through these inscriptions. I switched to scissors soon after.

As I grew older, I became obsessed with cuticle scissors. I was on a quest to find the perfect pair, which I once found. It had thin, long blades that allowed me to cut with the exact pressure and precision in both right and left hands. Miracle. On a visit to Beirut one summer, my mom noticed my scissors, recognized their unique qualities, and confiscated them on the spot. I could not say no. She, too, understood the importance of these tools that conjure up a whole history of care and violence, of grabbing and not letting go. But I soon replaced this pair with a better one. This one was short and had wide handles that looked like little ears that welcomed the fingers and kept them steady. It was made in Pakistan. With no brand name or model number, it managed to make its way to a market stand in New York, where I found it sandwiched between dentist and barber instruments. With time, this pair became wobbly, especially when I held it in my left hand, making the difficult task of cutting even more painful. Eventually, I learned that cuticles should not be cut at all. A metal or wood rod called a pusher should be used to put them back in their place. What a strange substance it is that infiltrates itself between the skin and the nail and ties them together. This thick, gelatinous seam exposes fraught connections between the finger and the nail, the past and the present, and countries and lovers. This seam, this ever-expanding border of the body, invites me today to crawl underneath the skin and retrieve a scene of love and separation.

The hand that grabbed mine as a child grabs me today, leaping through layers of pain and dead skin, forcing me to confront it all and tell the story of Bahieh (or Bahia).

She must have been sixteen when they smuggled her across the border. I see a pickup truck full of girls, going down a windy mountain road in the middle of the night. Domestic workers from poor villages along the Syrian coast, rocking their way to the glittering towns in the south. Yet the fastest road is neither mountainous nor windy but rather hugs the sea, connecting the cities of Baniyas and Tartus to Tripoli and Beirut. There are many crossing points from Syria to Lebanon: one goes over a river and has a different name on each side of the border. The other has an entire village situated in the no-man's-land between the two posts. In this murky landscape of identity and belonging, trafficking of humans and goods thrives as a way of life and as resistance to the colonial jigsaw that carved up the region after World War I.

With no papers, all that the girls in the truck held on to that night were memories of embraces and smells, and tastes and accents that would gradually dissipate as they settled into their new lives. They were destined to cook and clean and take care of children. Some would sleep on mattresses on the kitchen floor, others would have small rooms all to themselves—Beirut's version of the *chambre de bonne*, meaning maid's room. Child labor, indentured labor, domestic servitude . . . the categories fluctuate, but one thing is certain: these girls were forced into whatever their parents and handlers and customers had negotiated.

Some girls would eventually return to their villages to marry and have families of their own. And some would never again smell the sumac drying in the summer heat on their rooftops. In later years, these girls from Syria (but also from Egypt and other rural areas and refugee camps in Lebanon) would be replaced by ones from Sri Lanka, the Philippines, Ethiopia, and elsewhere. Syrian men would follow as well, part of an occupying army in the seventies and as a labor force in the nineties that came to rebuild the country in whose destruction they took part.

The woman who brought Bahieh to our house was called Lamia—Madame Lamia. She had an agency that provided domestic workers to Beiruti households. Her middleman, I imagine, must have paid the families small sums in exchange for their daughters' labor. Before bringing her to our house, Lamia placed Bahieh for a couple of years in the home of Wadih al-Safi, Lebanon's most iconic singer, a *bon-papa* (grandpa) figure beloved by the late Syrian president Hafez al-Assad. Al-Safi's most famous song, "Lebanon, Oh Piece of Heaven," makes people shiver and cry from longing. I'm not sure why Bahieh didn't stay with al-Safi's family too long, but she used to tell us stories about her time there, when she would ride bikes with his kids. They treated her well and she had a fond memory of it.

When Bahieh came to our house, she relieved my mom of her household chores and maternal duties. My mom put three conditions on my father before accepting his marriage proposal: "I don't enter the kitchen. I don't clean the house. I don't..." The third condition remained unsaid. It was about child-rearing, no doubt. I was born soon after Bahieh had arrived. They handed me over to her and convinced her that I was now her son, just like they had convinced my brothers and sister that my mom was now theirs. Parental swapping gone wild.

Photos from my childhood show Bahieh holding me with great pride and much affection. She had straight brown hair and hazel eyes. She was short and stubby. She was gentle and caring, but something about her in the photos is withdrawn. Some emotion is kept out of the frame in the pictures I have of her. Eventually, they bought her a camera and she became the official photographer of the entire family, and especially of me. She became my nanny.

The word for nanny in Arabic is *murabbia*. In Egypt, they call her *dada*, which is an old Turkish word that means grandma, nanny, or maid. No one in our household or among the neighbors and friends dared call her a maid. My parents were adamant. In their minds, she was a member of the family. My dad had used all his connections in Lebanon and Syria to get Bahieh a passport so that she could travel with us abroad. There were pictures of the two of us in London, feeding the pigeons in Trafalgar Square. Bahieh was the governess, British style. Her word was law. How could she possibly be the maid?

But pictures don't lie. Something about where she came from and how she came lingered, leaving a trace that the Kodak film and those other events of grabbing and cutting revealed.

One day, Madame Lamia—who must have been named after the child-eating monster in Greek mythology—came knocking at our door, wanting to take Bahieh away. She brought my nanny's older brother, who was called Hafez, just like the president of Syria back then. He didn't want her to work for people anymore, he claimed. Perhaps he wanted more money. Perhaps it was his mom back in the village who asked him to go fetch her. All I knew was that Lamia and Hafez had come to take my mother away. Hafez called her and asked her to pack her stuff. She refused. They argued. He slapped her. My dad ran for his gun. He wanted to shoot him. My mom screamed, "Adnan, let him be!"

They took her. I was barely one.

It was a scene from those movies that she and I would later watch in the theaters of Hamra. It was like the scene when Shahira dies, abandoning her son in the Egyptian movie *Azab Imraa* (A woman's pain). That's also why I cry every time I watch *The Sound of Music,* especially when the nanny Maria abandons the Von Trapp children, when they try to visit her in the monastery, and when she finally returns. Once I was in a relationship with an Austrian who looked just like one of those kids in the film. I stayed four years in that relationship because I got the chance to visit those mountains where Maria sang. I was looking for her in the majestic meadows cradled by the Alps.

My first memory, the first image to be inscribed on the screen of my mind like a daguerreotype, was formed when Bahieh was taken away. It was an abduction. The scene unfolded at the entrance of our apartment building. My sister is holding me while a taxi drives away. My nanny and her brother and the demonic Lamia are in that car. Though my childhood is documented in an extensive visual archive made up of pictures that Bahieh took, she couldn't have taken this picture that lingers in my memory.

Where does this image come from? Have I reconstituted it to mark that moment of abandonment? There is a link between the experience of loss and the birth of the image that I don't fully understand.

Bahieh couldn't bear our separation. She returned after forty days, that magic number that marks the end of mourning for people from our region. Perhaps she had tried to mourn but couldn't. In her exile, she stopped eating and lost interest in all things. Such is the case of separated lovers described in ancient manuals. Avicenna (Ibn Sina), the Muslim physician and polymath from the eleventh century, diagnosed this condition in his multivolume work *Canon on Medicine*, recommending talk therapy, a proper diet, and plenty of sleep. But how could she mourn he who was still waiting for her, refusing to be held by anyone else, even his own mother?

We want to believe in the power of mourning, but even Freud, somewhere in his essay on the subject, hinted that mourning is impossible.

Abandonment and reunion were a recurring theme throughout my childhood. My brothers and sister left for the U.S. and came back, and Bahieh would leave and return as well. But do they ever return? When she left for good in 1985, I was already a teenager. I didn't want her to leave, but then it was my capricious desire that didn't want to let go.

Within a year, the house was empty. It broke my father's heart and put an end to my childhood. Everyone understood that it was time for Bahieh to return to her village, find a husband, and have children of her own. She could no longer be our ward now that she was in her thirties. And I became too old to give out my hands for various experiments and little acts of cruelty.

So Bahieh went back to her village and married a man who had a motorcycle accident while serving in the army that left him broken. They had children together who went back and forth between Syria and Lebanon, fighting and working, and continuing a cycle that kept the borders of nations and of bodies permeable, craving something and someone on the other side, seeking impossible unions.

The Syrian president Hafez al-Assad, who ruled the country from 1971 until he bequeathed it to his son upon his death in 2000, firmly believed that the Lebanese and Syrians were ripped apart by borders and foreign conspiracies. He used to repeat the old phrase "one people in two countries." In fact, it was not until 2008 that the Syrian government recognized Lebanon's sovereignty and eventually opened an embassy in Beirut. The age-old dream of resurrecting greater

Syria that Arab nationalists used to brandish in the
face of colonial powers finally succumbed to international pressure in 2005. The assassination of Rafik
Hariri, Lebanon's former prime minister, forced Syrian troops to withdraw. The country that the Syrian
army entered in 1976 to fight in its civil war became
the troublesome child and tumultuous lover that had
to be released, abandoned, mourned. Syria was forced
to let go of this *part maudite*, this accursed part that
was ripped from its body, along with Alexandretta in
modern Turkey. But do you really ever let go?

Historians and geographers have always struggled
to identify the borders of Syria. In antiquity, Syria
comprised the coastal towns and the hinterland of the
Eastern Mediterranean. This is the land of the rising
sun, or the Levant, also known as *Bilad al-Sham*. As
the first-century Roman geographer Pliny the Elder
tells us,

> *Syria occupies the coast, once the greatest of lands,*
> *and is distinguished by many names; for the part*
> *which joins up to Arabia was formerly called*
> *Palæstina, Judæa, Cœle, and Phœnice. The country*
> *in the interior was called Damascena... Those who*
> *make a still more minute division of this country*
> *will have it that Phœnice is surrounded by Syria,*
> *and that first comes the maritime coast of Syria, part*
> *of which is Idumæa and Judæa, after that Phœnice,*
> *and then Syria. The whole of the tract of sea that*

lies in front of these shores is called the Phœnician Sea. The Phœnician people enjoy the glory of having been the inventors of letters, and the first discoverers of the sciences of astronomy, navigation, and the art of war.

Syria extended to the fabled city of Emessa, modern-day Homs, home of the high priest and Roman emperor Heliogabalus. This emperor danced for the sun god Baal fifteen hundred years before Louis XIV attempted his sun ballet. It also extended to the city of Palmyra. This was the home of Zenobia, the iconic queen who defied and threatened Roman dominance in the East and who was played by the Lebanese singer Fairuz in the Rahbani Brothers' musical play *Petra*.

Syria was at the heart of power struggles pitting Parthians and Romans, Ptolemies and Seleucids, who all fought on its territory. But what are its exact borders? Who will revive and bring it back as whole and one with itself across time? These are the kinds of questions that touch more on fantasy, as do all questions dealing with national identity and border demarcation in that ever-elusive Levant. It also shapes the relation between Syria and Lebanon today, that country where many claim descendance from those same Phoenicians that according to Pliny the Elder invented so many great things and were always surrounded by Syria.

Modern Lebanon was carved up from Mount Lebanon and greater Syria to include the Bekaa Valley and the coast of ancient Phoenicia. It started to emerge as a unified political entity following the conflict that ripped through the region in 1860. This conflict, which pitted Druze against Maronites, Muslims against Christians, was a turf and economic war as well as a sectarian conflict that would be reenacted in 1975. Back then, European powers intervened and granted Lebanon a special status within the Ottoman Empire. It was the beginning of Lebanon as we know it, the one that saw the light after World War I, when the Allies emerged victorious. French and British troops entered the land of the rising sun and carved it up along the Sykes–Picot agreement, sealing the collapse of the Ottoman Empire, delivering the coup de grâce to the "sick man of Europe." Lebanon and Syria would be administered by France until they reached "adulthood" and become their own independent states. They called this the mandate. But just as the fantasy of restoring greater Syria was wild, the fantasy of separation and independence seemed even harder to achieve.

Something about union and separation remains incomplete, pretending to be about borders and sovereignties when it is really about some leftover love or hatred or attachment that lingers, encroaches, erupts. It often appears in a gesture of withdrawal in some old photograph that becomes more visible with age.

———

The relation between Syria and Lebanon, involving ripping and trying to break free, carving up and cutting, was playing out in our household. As Bahieh was ripped from her family to go work in households in the mountains and cities of that glittering hub on the Mediterranean, I would experience, over and over, the tremors of this constant ripping and reuniting. This is the frame of those photographs that show a happy family with the nanny in the background that I took to my therapist when I first went to see her in New York in 2001. It is also the frame for those postcards of pine forests and mountains that Wadih al-Safi loved to sing about, and that Hafez al-Assad relished so much. Finally, it is the frame that allows me to grasp my relation to my mother, she who couldn't nurse or bathe or deal with milk, vomit, and diapers.

Bahieh became my mother. In fact, she often fought with my mom, accusing her of being selfish, uncaring, narcissistic. "What is this mother who only wants her son fed and dressed so that she can parade him in front of her friends and family like a trophy! What kind of mother only sees her son when he's all nice and clean, wearing vibrant colors that highlight his blue eyes so that they can reflect hers!" Bahieh told it like it was, yet my mom kept silent, recognizing the meager price she had to pay to have another woman raise her son. It was a Faustian pact my mother understood very well.

Bahieh fed and bathed, just like nannies and wet nurses in Arab culture ever since pre-Islamic times.

These nurses were called upon to breastfeed infants whose moms had just died or had no milk of their own. It was the custom of noble women from Mecca to send their newborns to go live with wet nurses in the desert for the first few years of their lives. It was thought that children developed stronger constitutions and acquired true Arab values if they grew up in a tribal encampment away from the urban sites of Arabia. It was a test of survival mixed with a romantic ideal. Perhaps this was a way for the mother not to get too attached to a child who might die in the early stages of life. Perhaps my mom wanted to shield herself from that eventuality, or from a divorce that would rip her son away.

A precarious border separates modern-day Beirut and pre-Islamic Mecca.

The Prophet Muhammad himself was sent to live in the desert for five years under the care of his wet nurse Halima, from the Bani Saad tribe. Halima breastfed the Prophet and raised him along with her own son, who became his "nursing brother." It is said that upon taking him in, Halima's milk flowed more fully, and so did the milk of the camel that nourished her little family. It is during this time in the wilderness that the early signs of Muhammad's prophecy appeared. Two angels came up to him one day, cut open his chest, extracted a black lump, and sewed him back up. They had thus purified him of original sin and laid the ground for his prophetic journey. When he told Halima of his encounter with the angels, she sought out his mother Amina in Mecca. His mother confirmed that while pregnant with him, she had dreamt that a light was coming out of her belly, illuminating the palaces of Syria, *al-Sham*, the land of the rising sun.

From the Arabian Desert to the palaces of Syria, the figure of the nanny or governess is associated with care and surrogacy when mothers are withdrawn, absent, unable to deal. This tradition continued into the medieval period and beyond. In *The Arabian Nights*, for instance, a nanny connected teenage lovers, carrying letters and offering advice on love and desire. This can also be observed in European culture and writings, where nannies became integral to plots and their twists. One need only remember the nurse in Shakespeare's *Romeo and Juliet* and the role that she played in uniting and dooming the lovers.

The girl from Syria continued this tradition as well, refining and developing it. With basic reading and writing skills, she learned French to help me with my homework. Once, she made me memorize the multiplication table, which was written on a large piece of paper and dotted with squares and colors. We shared the same room and the same mattress sometimes. She was my mom and my caretaker in a household that was full of love and conflict.

Every Saturday afternoon, Bahieh and I went out together. We would walk to Hamra Street, close to our house, to watch a movie. Indian, Egyptian, American... whatever was playing that day, it didn't matter. We watched it all. My repertoire of Egyptian films goes back to this era. Age appropriateness was never a question. Entrusted to the Syrian nanny, I grew up acquiring not so much the cultural values that pre-Islamic Meccans cherished so much, but rather an education in Egyptian popular culture.

Once, Bahieh took me to attend the filming of the show *Alam al-Sighar,* which means "children's world." The show's presenter was a famous TV personality, Maha Salma. Salma was a natural in front of the camera. She was always beautifully dressed and had long, wavy brown hair and impeccable makeup. The show aired every Saturday at six p.m., but we had to get to the station much earlier. Bahieh spoke to the producer of the show and told him that I should appear on stage and read a poem. The poem I had prepared that day was by the Lebanese Romantic poet Elias Abu-Shabaki. It went like this:

> *Oh sower of the field in the morn,*
> *Your life is evergreen.*
> *You are in the temple of flowers*
> *Like a philosopher deep in thought.*

I was very nervous when Maha Salma called on me to recite. Though I loved reciting poetry, and I was able to project with great ease in front of the entire class, sitting down on the floor surrounded by kids in front of cameras and blinding lights was not my ideal stage. I recited the poem and made no mistakes. When I was done, Maha Salma gave me a big hug, and the kids clapped.

Throughout the performance, Bahieh was standing across from the stage, reminding me of her presence. The poem that she had helped me memorize was about a place that we both knew very well. The fields to be sowed in the early morning were in her village in Syria, and with time I was destined to become that philosopher deep in thought. But for now, I was the Beiruti kid whose parents would drive him, along with his nanny, to spend a few weeks every summer in the Alawite heartland. This was Bahieh's break from household chores, but not from me.

My nanny's village is perched on the hills and mountains overlooking the coastal city of Baniyas, home to Syria's major oil refinery. The refinery, known as Misfat Baniyas, appears from the village as a cluster of stainless-steel pots that steam and simmer in the sun. As for her village, which is about ten miles up from the coast, it's called Al-Tun al-Marqab, not to be confused with the Markab or Marguat (the watchtower) fortress, located on a nearby hill. This fortress became the Syrian headquarters of the Hospitaller order in the twelfth century. Marguat resisted the siege of Saladin, who came to liberate the Levant from the Crusaders.

But my nanny's village was more beautiful and more important than any Crusader castle, near or far. In fact, the word *tun* is an old Turkic word that moved to Arabic and other languages, meaning "gold" or "the golden one."

In my nanny's golden village, they grew olives, figs, tobacco, sunflowers, apples, pears, and all that one could imagine in this type of landscape. By the end of the summer, rooftops were flush with drying fruits and vegetables and herbs ready for conservation. There were no refrigerators or electricity when I first started going to the village in the late seventies, so everything had to be dried and conserved in other ways for the long winter months. There were no paved roads or running water either. I learned to get the water from the well by throwing in a heavy metal bucket attached to a long chain. The bucket needed to hit the water at a certain angle to fill up. In the village I learned survival skills and techniques to manage water distribution and other chores that would come in handy when the situation worsened in Lebanon because of war and siege. I was ready.

All I wanted to do in the village was to ride donkeys. I loved donkeys. I used to call them my cousins. There were no riding saddles, just a thick cover (*hlaysi*), and a rope tied to the poor donkey's neck. Donkeys had no actual names, but were referred to according to their various attributes: the white one, the brown one, the short-eared one, et cetera. Riders had to carry a thick stick to tap the donkey on its mane to keep a steady pace. I also learned how to make the donkey gallop by pricking it in its withers. This gentle yet surgical prick made it rival any thoroughbred in gait and speed.

I rode donkeys and took cows out to graze. I even learned how to milk cows and goats by applying pressure to the nipples, pushing the milk down from the root to the little orifice from which the liquid spurts out. I drank the milk and learned the dialect of the village, which I can still speak to this day. I even teased my nanny by calling her Bahi, saying her name in the village accent, which she hated. She always yelled at me when I spoke "like them." The conversion to a Beiruti sophisticate was well underway for her, while I was becoming a true village urchin.

I also learned about the ruling Baath party by watching TV and playing with the kids in the village. They all attended the camps of an organization called the Baath Vanguards. I gradually memorized their songs, especially the Baath party anthem:

Oh Arab Youth
Begin your march
And raise your voice up high:
Long live the Arab Baath!

The anthem's call for Arab youth to unite around the Baath, which I also heard on TV every night, scared and excited me. And I developed a peculiar understanding of the anthem's lyrics: I heard the word for voice, *sawt*, as *sawt* with a softer *s*, which means whip. *Sawt qawiy*, which means strong voice, transformed in my mind to "strong whip." Now, this mistranslation brings to mind that scene from *Lawrence of Arabia* where Lawrence, played by Peter O'Toole, gets arrested by the Ottomans in Daraa, Syria. When he refuses the sexual advances of the officer, the soldiers lay him on a bench, tear his shirt off, and whip him on the back. His gaze in that scene betrays complex emotions, a mix of pain and pleasure that will define Arab nationalism and forever mark the imagination of the little boy with a Syrian nanny. It was as if Lawrence was being punished for desiring those Arabs and championing their cause and that of the future Baath Vanguards.

At one point, I became friends with an older boy in the village called Juwad. I was around ten, while he was well into his teenage years. *Juwad* means rider or knight in Arabic. He had beautiful green eyes and light-brownish hair that he combed to the right, in the sixties fashion. Juwad took an interest in me. We would sit on the rooftop of the house of his brother, who worked for the *mukhabarat* or the Syrian Secret Service and was serving in Lebanon. We would sit under that makeshift tent made of dead branches to offer shade like a *sukkah*, drink yerba maté, and talk into the night. Once I asked him to show me his back. I explained that this would seal our friendship, tie our bond forever. He was surprised and somewhat incredulous at my request, but he played along. We were alone in his brother's house. He turned his back toward me, bent over, and slowly lifted his tank top. It was a moment of revelation. I saw that glistening back, so smooth and sensual, staring at me, offering itself to my dreams and fantasies for years to come.

Juwad would take me with him to hang out with the other young men in the village. These boys were curious about me, about my family's political affiliation, and whether we approved of Syria's involvement in Lebanon. One of the more boisterous boys, Ashraf, once asked me what I thought of Ghazi Kanaan, the Syrian general ruling Lebanon at the time. "Isn't he a man!?" (*mu rijial*), meaning a mensch. I responded immediately, "What did you think he was, an animal?" (*shu lakan hayawen*). The guys laughed, but Ashraf felt rebuffed. He could have denounced me, and I could have been whisked away and made to disappear for having spoken ill of Syria's viceroy. Slowly he laughed. It was a nervous laughter, as if to disavow my response or avoid having to confront the Beiruti kid, who was now the son of one of theirs. I would never be taunted about politics again. And I understood that these Baath Vanguards were part of a tribe to which I had become attached through my nanny. It was a tribe I feared and desired; it offered me protection and care but had the power to punish and torture me.

She was doing the dishes. I came from behind and poked her with my finger. I was five or six. I don't know what came over me. Perhaps I wanted to be swallowed by that butt protruding from her tight jeans. Perhaps I wanted to return to the womb of this girl who raised me, to get in from the backdoor of motherhood.

She swiftly turned around with the brush in one hand and a saw knife in the other. She slashed me. She didn't mean to, but she did. The blood started gushing from my right hand, on my knuckle, at the foot of my little finger. My dad stitched it with the extra-thick thread used for C-sections—all that he could find in his kit that day. No anesthesia. My mom blew on the wound as he sewed me up in their bedroom. They were consoling me. No words were uttered. No words could explain what happened, what I had experienced that day. I still feel the burning pain of needles and knives.

The scar on my right hand is visible to this day. It looks like the window of a small house in an idyllic village overlooking the Mediterranean. During my childhood, the scar allowed me to recognize my right from my left. It also gave my right hand the strength to handle the cuticle scissors more steadily, no matter how old and wobbly they got. This gave me the power to cut the dead skin with great precision, to avoid spilling blood, and to tell the story of the girl from Syria.

Did I mention that "cutting" and "storytelling" are the same word in Arabic (*qass*)?

There is something about the story of the wound, about the incision and the scar that make it visible, painful, tolerable, that needs to be told. The cutting is about Lebanon and Syria, my nanny and me, and about love and violence and stories that explain relationships and make legible echoes and accents from the past, from that golden village of my childhood.

The last time I saw my nanny was in 2002. I visited her with a friend from the U.S., an anthropologist who had come in order to understand something about Lebanon and Syria and me. He took the last picture of the two of us together. In the picture, she is wearing a T-shirt with the image of a wolf with a cheeky smile. It looks like a caricature of the wolf from *Little Red Riding Hood*. I am wearing a green T-shirt with an inscription that reads "Not all who wander are lost." It sounds like the statements uttered by prophets about those who were lost in the wilderness. The wolf on her shirt is tapping the head of a little boy with a cap.

She looks a little withdrawn in this picture as well, as if she is controlling some feeling of pleasure at having seen me after all these years. While I look glowing, ecstatic to be reunited with her for what would be the last time.

No matter all the cutting and scarring, in the end, not all wolves devour little children. Lest we forget that a she-wolf served as a wet nurse to Romulus and Remus, the founders of Rome. Wet nurses and nannies crossed borders and deserts and the animal-human divide to be with the children who were chosen for them and whom they loved and chose at the end. A similar crossing in the back of a pickup truck allowed me to be who I am today, *ibn Bahieh*, the son of the girl from Syria.

8

THE FISH TANK

Orange. White. Red. Black. White with orange spots. White with red spots. Black with bulging eyes. Orange with puffy chin. A dozen or so of them. Going round and round and up and down. Reacting to motion and light and food. Little flakes dropped once or twice a day float on the surface, causing such commotion in that little tank.

It was a medium-size, rectangular tank that my parents had gotten me a few years back, after one of those stellar grade reports. I came home one day and found them on a stand in the living room, my new little friends. I remember decorating the tank with a large piece of dried coral and little shells that I had collected from the beach. At the end, the tank looked homey, all that the fish needed to play and swim free.

But with time, I started missing some of them. Where is the orange one with puffy cheeks? And the Black Moor had disappeared. Where did they go? One day, as I was cleaning the tank with my nanny, we took the white coral out and found the missing fish stuck between its tips, deep inside. The coral had turned into a trap that was closing in on my goldfish, cutting them with its razor tips and holding them hostage in its belly. Though dead, the coral came to life in that tank as a monstrous creature, preying on the little ones as if seeking revenge. Eventually, they all died, and my parents never got me fish again.

With its original inhabitants gone, the tank and its water filtration system and decorative shells were put in the attic and almost forgotten. No one knew that it was going to house a new band of colorful fellas. No one knew that these residents would be refugees, escaping from another tank in another house that was soon to be consumed by the whims of siege and war.

The new school that would settle in my tank belonged to my cousin. He, his brother, and their mom lived in Verdun, the neighborhood not far from ours where my own school was located. Their dad, who was originally Syrian, worked in Saudi Arabia. One day, we woke up to my aunt's frantic call: she had heard that an Israeli commando was going to attack their building to abduct a cadre of the Palestine Liberation Organization who lived there. They needed to evacuate immediately.

How did she hear this rumor? Was it true? I started imagining the commando landing in a helicopter on the rooftop of my aunt's building. I started seeing the soldiers dangling from ropes and crashing through glass windows, which would send splinters flying everywhere. I must have seen this in a movie. Not that such commando operations were uncommon in Beirut at the time, especially not in that neighborhood.

My aunt and her kids packed their bags and came to stay in an empty apartment in our building that belonged to another aunt, who had already left town.

I remember when they first arrived. My cousin who is around my age or slightly older was carrying a big plastic bucket. Water was scarce, I knew that, but I wondered why he was carrying this wide bucket, wrapping his arms around it like a mother embracing her child. When I came closer, I discovered his goldfish, resembling those I had a few years back. He brought them with him. They needed to be saved, too, from the Israeli commando threatening to invade their building.

My aunt and her kids stayed in our building for a few weeks. During that time, my cousin and I watched the World Cup that was taking place in Spain. It was summer 1982. With no electricity, we struggled to find a battery-powered TV to watch the games, especially the finale. He supported the Italians, I think, or was it the Germans? The Italians were the most stylish. Even their game was elegant. Clean, smooth

passes translated into beautiful goals that earned them
the championship. But I was more interested in playing than watching soccer, especially when it's on a
small black-and-white screen. Besides, there was a
different game unfolding outside, with teams at each
other's throats and no referee to slap them with yellow
or red cards.

Like many people that summer, my aunt and her
kids eventually left the city. She managed to get a
taxi to Damascus and from there flew to London to
meet up with her husband. Before leaving, my cousin
made me the caretaker of his goldfish. Now it was my
turn to wrap my arms around them and protect them
from war. But I had failed in that task before. And the
worsening conflict that summer was eroding whatever concentration and care were left in me.

I accepted the charge. I had no choice. I got the
old tank out, cleaned it up, and made it comfy for the
new residents. The old coral was not welcome this
time around. The fish didn't need to worry about getting stuck as they made their daily circles and ran to
the surface to nibble the few flakes dropped by their
foster dad.

But there were events that would disturb the peace
of the fish tank and alter its chemistry, changing the
lives of its inhabitants and of those caring for them
forever.

———

In the summer of 1982, Israel invaded Lebanon
with the stated objective of kicking out Palestinian
leader Yasser Arafat and his fighters. It was an atro-
cious summer. Daily bombardment of West Beirut,
where we lived and where Arafat and the PLO were
based. Rockets and shells rained down from air, land,
and sea. The Israeli army and their allies, a militia con-
glomerate controlling East Beirut called the Lebanese
Forces, had encircled West Beirut. This is the scene
of Palestinian poet Mahmoud Darwish's collection
Memory for Forgetfulness: August, Beirut, 1982. Darwish
lived in Caracas, a neighborhood by the sea that was
particularly exposed to the fire of Israeli warships.

Beirut was being bombed to the ground, forced
to capitulate once and for all, renounce its title as the
Arab capital of resistance when other capitals had
withdrawn from the military confrontation with
Israel. Beirut was the last bastion against a peace that
was being forged by the barrel of the gun.

But we stayed put. We struggled as best as we
could to keep our home and our life going. There was
no electricity or water, food was running out, and
even the oxygen in the air was thinning out from all
the smoke and rubble. As one official of the Lebanese
Forces put it in a *Washington Post* interview from that
time, "I believe the Israelis will take the PLO militar-
ily, just as they have begun to do now—slice by slice.
They will push the PLO deeper and deeper into West
Beirut, like they were squeezing a lemon." Everyone

in West Beirut that summer felt pushed deeper and deeper, squeezed, drained of their lives and livelihoods, day by day, drop by drop.

I remember a convoy of humanitarian aid that managed to enter our enclave. It was a gift from the "Servant of the Two Holy Shrines" of Islam: Mecca and Medina. Khadim al-Haramen al-Sharifen was the honorific title bestowed upon the Saudi king who was sending us bags of rice, sugar, and other food items. The lorry parked in front of our building, and people gathered in the back, eager to receive the boxes of food.

I remember the boxes' confusing inscription: *hiba min Khadim al-Haramen al-Sharifen* (a gift from the Servant of the Two Holy Shrines). I heard that it was the king of Saudi Arabia who had sent us food, but who is this servant and what are these shrines? Jokes started to go around, with people wondering why the Saudis would send us two blankets and two sheets in the middle of summer. The kids were playing on the words *haramen al-sharifen* (the two holy shrines), turning them into *hremen w-sharshafen* (two blankets and two sheets). Humor is often deployed to make the horror of war and siege bearable. Ungrateful Beirutis!

With school in recess and unable to venture far from our living quarters, the other kids in the building and I played in the parking lot. We played soccer, dodgeball, hopscotch, and *sabaa hjara* (seven stones), a game that consisted of knocking out a tower of stones with a tennis ball. One day, an NGO came to the neighborhood and launched a series of activities to keep the kids engaged. They summoned us to the offices of the Women's Council, which was in the building adjacent to ours. They sat us at long rectangular tables and led us through activities involving painting and drawing, stitching and gluing. I couldn't concentrate. I started teasing the doorman's daughters, with whom I used to play. The whole thing felt weird, unreal, artificial. Why were we in the Women's Council and not outside playing? Who could concentrate on gluing? I couldn't stay put.

We woke up one morning to the news that West Beirut was being subjected to the most intense bombardment since the beginning of the invasion. Describing that day in his collection of prose poems on the siege, Mahmoud Darwish wrote:

> *The dawn made of lead is still advancing from the direction of the sea, riding on sounds I haven't heard before. The sea has been entirely packed into stray shells. It is changing its marine nature and turning into metal. Does death have all these names?*

Darwish later dubbed that day Beirut's Hiroshima. It was August 6, 1982. We could hear the missiles and rockets exploding closer and closer. At one point, we felt an indescribable pressure, a pressure that went into our bodies and pierced our ears. It was like nothing we had heard or experienced before. At the time, my brothers and dad were out buying food. The Akar Building, located a few blocks from ours, was hit and flattened by a thermobaric bomb.

Better known as a vacuum bomb, a thermobaric bomb uses a two-staged explosion. After detonation, the first stage sets off a cloud of ignitable fuel, which can easily penetrate open space. The second stage ignites the cloud, resulting in a long-lasting, large-volume fireball that can evaporate bodies in proximity, as well as create devastating pressure waves and vacuums that suck the oxygen from the air and rupture internal organs. The sheer power and extent of a thermobaric explosion, when set off inside urban environments, guarantees large-scale civilian loss of life and the destruction of key infrastructure.

There are reports that the vacuum bomb was used by Nazi Germany in World War II, the United States in Vietnam and Afghanistan, and Russia in Chechnya and Ukraine. In the face of this monster weapon, the seven-story steel and concrete building that had been squatted in by Palestinian refugees stood no chance. It collapsed in one blow, killing everyone inside.

It was rumored that Arafat himself had been in the building just a few minutes before it was bombed. Someone must have provided the intelligence that led to the strike. But Arafat had nine lives. It seems that he was born with part of an amniotic sac (*burquu*) wrapped around his face. This is what doctors call an "en caul birth." This face cover is believed to be a sign of divine immunity and inner vision. Arafat escaped unscathed.

The worst thing during the war was missing a family member when fighting broke out or an explosion was heard. The feeling that someone might be unaccounted for in those moments was terrifying. So the minute my dad and brothers came back home that day, we all felt relieved and huddled together in my parents' room. As we were all gathered, another explosion of a different kind turned the sky gray, flipped the curtains, and threw us all from our seats.

My brother, who was sitting on a chair by the window, landed in the hallway some twenty feet away. I was on the bed. I flew to the side and found my dad landing on top of me. Screams filled the room. It was apocalyptic, the closest we had come to dying during the fifteen-year conflict. Miraculously, no one was hurt.

A missile launched by an Israeli warship—we later learned—landed only a couple of feet from our building, right beneath my parents' room. The crater that the missile produced might as well have been caused by a meteorite. These meteorites fell like artillery of heaven, terrifying people and strengthening their faith in a higher power that manifested itself through shock and awe. In Islam, a piece of meteorite called the black stone is exposed by the Kaaba in Mecca.

When visiting the shrine, pilgrims take turns touching it to receive its blessings.

The inscription on the boxes of food sent by the servant of the Muslim holy shrines was a foreshadowing of a meteorite launched from an Israeli warship that almost wiped us out that summer. It was a sign that we needed to heed. We swallowed our pride and went down to the shelter for the first time.

Most buildings in Beirut had a basement that was often used as a *dépôt* (warehouse). With the onset of the war, the word *maljaa* (shelter) soon replaced *dépôt* to refer to this floor. In our building, the *dépôt* was rented out to a printing company. When we went down that day, we discovered stacks of dusty notebooks littering the basement's staircase and hallways. We had to walk around them to reach a dark, open space.

I remember staring into the darkness and feeling cold, unwelcome. We and a few neighbors were there only briefly, as if we had to go down to check it out, as if we had to pretend that there was a shelter when none existed.

But there was something else we needed to see in that basement, something deep within us. Thinking about it today, the dusty towers of notebooks were welcoming us to the kingdom of the dead. They were like the pillar of salt into which Lot's wife had turned upon looking back at Sodom. Discovering those pillars made us realize that the punishment raining down from the heavens had befallen us a long time ago. This inhospitable shelter held a mirror to our faces. The past and the future appeared in these stacks of paper and bone that were also ours. No one was going to survive this war, no one was going to make it out alive.

We left immediately and never went down to the shelter again.

After a few months of one of the worst sieges in modern history, and one that turned the city into a wasteland, an agreement was reached. When Arafat and his supporters recognized that they were completely squeezed, they decided to leave Beirut. While the Israeli army committed not to enter the city, the various factions agreed to support Israel's ally and head of the Lebanese Forces, Bashir Gemayel, in his quest to become the next president of Lebanon.

The cannons fell silent. Arafat and his fighters boarded the *Atlantis* and set sail for Greece, and from there to Tunisia. The photographer Fouad El Khoury, who was in Beirut documenting the invasion, took a famous picture of Arafat on the cruise ship during the crossing. The picture shows Arafat from behind, with his arms laid on the deck's railing, gazing at the horizon. We can see his iconic kaffiyeh descending from his head down to his shoulders and back, mimicking in its movement the map of Palestine. Behind him was a site of ruins. Like Lot, he did not look back.

———

As Arafat was leaving Beirut, my family decided to take a break of its own and head to London and Paris for a few weeks. We needed a vacation. But Bahieh, my nanny, didn't want to travel with us. She and I had accompanied my parents to London the year before and got terribly bored. I remember arriving at Heathrow aboard the Lebanese carrier Middle East Airlines. When the plane landed, it headed to an isolated spot in the airport. As we disembarked and started to make our way down the stairs, I saw soldiers, barricaded behind sandbags and pointing their guns at us. It was the early eighties, and commando operations of all sorts were in fashion. I was shocked at this sight. Did we really land in London? Yes, it is London, my dear, *Only in London*—as author Hanan al-Shaykh would later title her novel about the city. London, the capital of shopping, parks, and castles. And there was the zoo as well, and the pigeons at Trafalgar Square that I loved to feed. But my nanny and me, who didn't speak English, got so bored after a couple of weeks that my parents decided to put us on a plane back to Lebanon by ourselves. With my French and the few English words I had picked up, we managed to find our way through Heathrow and head back to Beirut.

London was calling, but my nanny was adamant: she wasn't going there again. And I didn't want to leave her by herself. I couldn't bear it. My parents agreed that I would stay behind and asked me what

I wanted as a reward for my continued resistance in West Beirut. *Patins* (roller skates), I answered. Bahieh took me to a shop by our house and asked me to choose a pair. The skates I chose looked like those from the movies with skating rinks and disco music and crazy lights. The skates were white and had red and blue stripes that shone in the dark. They were my first real skates. I had to survive a war and a state of siege to get them. But it was worth it: I was going to stay with Bahieh, we'd have the house to ourselves, and I'd skate the war away.

But the day my father went to buy the tickets, I had a change of heart. I panicked. I got scared to be apart from my family after all the huddling and close calls. Perhaps it was an early sign of my FOMO, which would get worse with age. Though my love for Bahieh knew no bounds, the idea of having all my family travel and leave me behind terrified me. My dad had already left the house. When I decided to travel with them, someone at home called the ticket agent to let my dad know. I still remember the anxiety I felt wondering whether my dad had gotten the message or not. In my mind, I was recanting: "No, I'm not Bahieh's son, I'm your son, don't leave me! I want to go!" Thinking about it today, I wonder if I had really wanted both, the roller skates and the trip abroad. And I got exactly that.

A few days later, we were on our way. Beirut's airport was still closed, so we took a taxi to Damascus, spent the night there, and flew to London the next morning. That night in Damascus, I went into my brothers' hotel room. They were watching a film about a man who survives in the Nordic wilderness. There was snow and rivers and streams and fur. Thinking about it today, it reminds me of the film *The Revenant*, with Leonardo DiCaprio, which is about the fur trade and savagery and the obstinate will for survival. Man against nature and a sign of things to come.

During the war, the Lebanese who were able to leave the country went all over. Some settled in London or Paris, some went back and forth, and some went as close as Cyprus, which we visited often. There were also some who went as far as the United States or even Australia. And when parents couldn't leave, kids were plucked from schools at the age of fifteen and sixteen and sent to live with an aunt or an uncle abroad to prevent them from being recruited by one militia or the other. A friend of mine ended up with his aunt in East Tennessee. Moving from the French system to the American one in a forced transition that lasted barely a month, he ended up going to college there before ultimately moving to New York.

I would be shipped out as well, sent to Côte d'Ivoire at the age of sixteen, but for now London was calling, and I needed to practice my English and confront anxieties that far exceeded those of war.

Many of my parents' friends and cousins settled in London. They lived in South Kensington, Knightsbridge, and Richmond, areas I got to know very well as a kid. I tagged along wherever my parents went. I went shopping with my mom in big department stores that caused me a great deal of stress. My ultimate terror was the fear of getting lost. She would ask me to grab her dress and not let go. Of course, this was an unrealistic proposition, as she would be browsing and trying on clothes for hours on end. I lost her once. Unable to see through the aisles of hanging clothes, I crawled on the floor and started looking from below, trying to recognize her from her shoes and the hem of her dress.

Images of shoes and legs come crashing into my memory, while my heart races as I recall the fear of losing her.

Once she was pickpocketed. Looking down at her purse, she realized that it was open. The cash was gone. I started yelling, "Police, Police!" To no avail. We had to use the few coins I had to get us on the double-decker back to the hotel that day.

My memory of London as a child had many bright spots as well, including rowing on the Serpentine, the lake inside Hyde Park. There was something about rowing on that small lake that calmed me and extracted me from the bustle of Oxford Street and its department stores. The repetitive strokes of the oars brought me back to Beirut, to the beach, and to my little inflatable boat that I would take out every day during the summer.

And then of course there was British food. We bought tasteless fish fingers and fruits and vegetables from the supermarket across from the hotel. That's why when I read the work of Ahmad Faris al-Shidyaq, the Lebanese scholar who lived in Britain in the nineteenth century, I immediately related to his multiple outbursts against the food and scarcity of good produce. But by the early eighties, thank God, McDonald's was widely available in the UK. I ended up living on Big Macs and strawberry milkshakes. In fact, for a long time I thought that McDonald's was a British chain, with its flagship store located on Oxford Street. The burgers were served in pink-and-green Styrofoam boxes that unfolded to make room for the fries. By the end of that trip, I was a little overweight (*surpoids*). This was the diagnosis of the nutritionist that my dad took me to see when we got back to Beirut. She put me on a diet, allowing me to have four candies a week and lunch with the family on Sunday.

There was another source of heavy and yummy food that contributed to my excess weight that summer. My father had friends from Kuwait and Qatar who had houses in London and who invited us for sumptuous meals. In these feasts one could find dates from the Arabian Peninsula, pistachios from Iran, Indian rice and spices, and lamb, lamb, and more lamb. Food and utensils were flown in to adorn their spreads. Big rice-and-meat platters covered with fried nuts were laid on tables or on the floor.

Once, we sat around a huge stainless-steel platter. I watched as each guest reached for the succulent rice and meat, learning how to make little balls of the sticky rice and then hurling them in my mouth like a penguin catching a fish at London Zoo. For someone who was taught at an early age to handle his fork and knife in preparation for a career in surgery just like his dad, this curling and hurling shocked and amused me. But while we were curling and hurling that summer, an event was about to shatter our break from war and cast an indelible blotch on humanity's conscience. More personally, I was going to experience the fear of losing the woman who raised me and who was left to face alone the savagery that was about to overtake Beirut.

One day, I woke up in our hotel room in London to the anguished voices of my parents. My dad's face was grim, and my mom was crying. There were images of an explosion on TV. A big blast followed by tanks and soldiers on the move. Did the war start again? My mom explained to me what was happening as I was waking up. My eyes were still half-closed, and my head was slowly coming into its upright position.

They had killed Lebanon's newly elected president, Bashir Gemayel. And there is more. A princess died. No, not Diana. Not yet at least. Another princess, the actress Grace Kelly. She had died in a car crash off the hills of Monaco.

Grace and Bashir, two stars, two magnetic figures who galvanized audiences and generated much fantasy, gone in one day. Political and romantic ideals shattered. And our vacation, our little break from war, shattered along with it. The Israeli army that was besieging West Beirut decided to enter the city. We were now stuck in London, not knowing when or if we could return.

And what about Bahieh? She was all by herself in that apartment in Beirut. Would I ever see her again?

At the hotel where we stayed, I slept on a foldable bed that my parents had requested be brought into their room. I would always sleep on those beds whenever just the three of us stayed in hotels. After my siblings left the house in the mideighties, my parents and I used to spend weekends in some hotel somewhere, meeting up with friends and relatives in the mountains or up the coast in Lebanon. This foldable bed was always there for me, crowding and dividing the room no matter how big or small it was.

As a child, I used to sleep with my mom in her bed. My nanny slept next to me on a mattress on the floor. Eventually, when my mom remodeled the house and started sharing a room with my dad again, my parents would ask me to join them for their afternoon nap. I could never nap. When they brought me into their bed, I felt trapped. Each pulled the cover to his or her side, leaving me in what looked more like a ditch or a trench. It was an unbearable feeling. I had to wait for the right moment to ask one of them to move over so I could break free. Thinking about it today, I see myself lying there like a soldier from World War I who has inadvertently fallen into an enemy trench. He needs to escape before getting noticed. In the meantime, he plays dead, pretending to be a statue, a sandbag like the ones used to divide a city and a household where fights would often lead to divorce and custody battle threats.

It was September 14, 1982. It was my mother's birthday and the day commemorated by Christians as the Exaltation of the Holy Cross (Eid al-Salib). This event marks the transformation of the cross from an instrument of torture into divine symbol, a life-giving tree that radiates hope and salvation for all humanity. But that day we were in that hotel room in London, processing the news about Bashir Gemayel and Grace Kelly. There will be no birthday for my mom and no exaltation either.

That afternoon, when my parents took their nap, I got up, went to the bathroom, reached for my mom's scissors, and started cutting my eyelashes.

The scene is silent. Almost mechanical. I'm not sure what devil possessed my hand. I was staring at myself in the mirror above the sink as I brought the scissors to my eye. I was observing myself, as if expecting something to happen, waiting for some reaction or blink or emotion that was nowhere to be found. I cut the eyelashes on my left eye. I don't know why I did it. I was bored. I didn't want to nap with them, and I couldn't go out on my own. I was stuck in that room, not knowing what to do with myself.

It was the hour of abandonment. An action, any action, needed to break my restlessness, even if it had no meaning, no purpose, no cause.

When my parents woke up, I told them what I had done. They were shocked, confused, horrified. As if the news of the day were not horrible enough. What was I cutting? Why my eyelashes? Was this the barbed wire protecting the trench in which I had fallen? I vividly remember the cold-bloodedness with which I brought the scissors to my eye. A determination overcame me in this hour of the day when their two bodies came together, and I had to play dead.

Bashir Gemayel was a young and charismatic leader. Even his enemies thought so. He was the scion of a political family in Lebanon that fanned nationalist feelings and proclaimed Lebanon for the Lebanese only. His speeches included declarations like "Our battle is about sovereignty and independence, and all the Lebanese should take part in this battle." These powerful words galvanized audiences, but didn't always correspond to the practices and ideologies that his party was pursuing.

In 1937, a year after their founding by Bashir's father, Pierre Gemayel, the Kataeb Party, or the Phalanges, paraded in Beirut wearing puffy black pants and white gloves, raising their hands in salute to the leader and looking like a squad of fashionistas overtaking the city streets. The style was Italian, for sure, and the ideology Spanish. Pierre Gemayel had brought it all back from the Berlin Olympics, in which he had participated as the captain of the Lebanese soccer team in 1936. He must have been impressed by the pomp and circumstance. And all these flags!

With Il Duce, the Caudillo, and the Führer in the mix, the puffy pants gradually gave way to khaki ones and military fatigues, and the Phalanges squad turned into a militia and an army that was integrated by 1982 into what became known as the Lebanese Forces. They eventually went to war against the Palestinians and their supporters, dragging the country into a fifteen-year-old conflict. I guess they wanted to preserve Lebanon's identity and independence, no matter what crises spilled over in the region. For them, Lebanon was only for those who happened to have been living on the right side of the border when Mr. Sykes and M. Picot drew their map in 1916 and enforced it on the ground following the Allies' victory. The Phalanges saw Lebanon as an oasis in a desert of chaos and backwardness. This blessed country stretched back to the time of the Phoenicians, from whom they claimed descent. All those who did not belong needed to be kicked out, no matter what the means.

The Lebanese Forces were the main faction controlling East Beirut and supporting the Israelis against
the Palestinians in Lebanon. The enemy of my enemy
is my friend, even if this new friend ends up occupying my land afterward. So when the Israeli army
invaded in 1982, it set up headquarters in East Beirut
to coordinate its onslaught on the western enclave of
the city, the bastion of Arab causes and regimes.

Petrodollars and AK-47s, and bags of sugar and
rice poured into West Beirut to bolster the resistance
against imperialism and Israel. Ideology turned kids
to cannon fodder in a conflict that brought the Cold
War and other global confrontations to our streets,
our doorsteps, inside our homes. But no amount of
rice and sugar can stand in the face of Merkava tanks
and F-16 fighter jets, and warships and submarines.

Eventually, West Beirut was brought to its knees. A
truce that required the expulsion of Arafat and his supporters was signed. Shortly after, the Lebanese parlia-
ment met and elected Bashir Gemayel as the president
of Lebanon. All seemed to be going as planned. The
Right had won. The Left that had descended on Lebanon from all corners of the world—and that included
groups like the Japanese Red Army and the German
Baader-Meinhof Gang—had to pack and leave, along
with Arafat and his merry men. It was Spain all over
again, a Beiruti *Farewell to Arms.* But not quite.

After the capitulation of the anti-imperialists, a
bomb went off. It was a timed bomb that tore through

the heart of the winning faction, shattering their dream of victory. Gemayel was assassinated on a visit to his party's headquarters. He came riding to the presidency on the corpses of those who were crushed in flattened buildings, only to meet a similar end. The images of the explosion showed him being pulled from a building where flesh and steel intermingled to create a new matter, unleash old monsters. This would be the fate of many leaders after him as well. But for now, it was time for revenge, and it would be horrific.

As the Israeli army entered West Beirut, Gemayel's Lebanese Forces entered the Palestinian refugee camps of Sabra and Shatila to drink the blood of those who resisted their prodigal son. It didn't matter whether they were the ones responsible for his death or not, whether they were armed or not. The son who wanted Lebanon for the Lebanese was going to be avenged by eliminating those who were not. The Palestinians in the camps were under the protection of the international community and UN forces that withdrew following the assassination of Gemayel. The massacre, which lasted for two days, was perpetrated by a bloodthirsty army that decided to exterminate the city that had rebuffed them.

They piled up bodies like pyramids. It was Jerusalem of the first Crusade all over again.

We were stuck in London. We were horrified and devastated as we saw the images coming out of

Lebanon on TV. A newscast showed street fighting in what looked like our neighborhood. When I saw this, all I could think of was my nanny, all alone in our apartment in Beirut, trapped like a goldfish in a tank. What if they came for her? She is Syrian, after all. What if I return and find her disemboweled, like in those images from the camps? They were in our neighborhood, I thought, closing in on her.

I had to reach her. I started calling frantically. I sat by a rotary dial phone at my aunt's apartment in London, turning the dial, turning the wheel that would decide whether Bahieh would live or not. The phone was on a stand near the entrance of their apartment. My parents were in the living room discussing the developments in Lebanon while I dialed away.

After minutes if not hours of dialing, my index finger turned red, scorched from the little round crevices where it had inserted itself, moving the dial to the right, waiting for it to settle, and then moving it to the right again and again. It felt as if I were sharpening my finger in those little holes. With every stroke my finger was morphing into a pencil that needed to write a letter in a language that was now broken, on paper stacked like bones in the catacomb of war.

With every turn of the dial, the holes would shave away a layer of my skin that was now offered to her, over there, in exchange for her safety. This finger, which she had cut in the past, was turning like a whirling dervish in a hopeless quest to reach her.

At that moment, I wished that the phone could suck me into its metal and plastic wiring like a vibration, a murmur that would travel through the power of magnets and electricity to meet her on the other side. I needed to reach her.

I was turning that dial to turn back time, to return to the moment that preceded Gemayel's assassination, that preceded the Israeli army's entering the city, that preceded my decision to travel and leave her behind. I was like those gods from antiquity who recanted their vengeful plot, who sought to undo it with every turn of the dial.

Communing with my instrument of torture in that hallway, I entered a trance that numbed my body, my pain, and the guilt I was feeling for not being there with her. But no matter how much I tried, I couldn't get through. It was as if the savagery that was unleashed upon Gemayel's assassination had taken hold of my body, emptying my actions of any logic or causality. Thinking about it today, I see my body like that of a marionette, moving with strings that dangled from a realm above, in the heavens, those same heavens that rained down projectiles and missiles but never salvation.

The tree of life was barren, and the heavens were relentless in their vengeance.

That summer, I took great care of the goldfish that my cousin left behind. He saved them from an Israeli

commando operation that would have either killed
them on the spot or put them on trial as terrorists,
working for a Syrian agent in West Beirut. He saved
them from certain death and from a sham trial where
the "freedom fighting" argument of the defense would
have fallen on deaf ears. But nothing withstands the
trial of a siege that slowly but surely nibbles away at
essential goods, nutrients, and air itself.

Soon enough, the food that my cousin had left for
his goldfish would start to run out. Where could we
get more food? No pet stores were open, and we knew
no one who had goldfish at the time. I was horrified.
It was the hour I had feared would come, the hour that
would expose the void in me, the vacuum in all of us,
our unmotherhood. The monstrous coral was going to
awaken once more and seek vengeance on my foster
fish. The coral was transforming into Lady Macbeth,
howling in the attic where I had locked it up:

> *The raven himself is hoarse*
> *That croaks the fatal entrance of Duncan*
> *Under my battlements. Come, you spirits*
> *That tend on mortal thoughts, unsex me here,*
> *And fill me from the crown to the toe top-full*
> *Of direst cruelty. Make thick my blood,*
> *Stop up th'access and passage to remorse,*
> *That no compunctious visitings of nature*
> *Shake my fell purpose, nor keep peace between*
> *Th' effect and it. Come to my woman's breasts,*

And take my milk for gall, you murd'ring ministers,
Wherever in your sightless substances
You wait on nature's mischief. Come, thick night,
And pall thee in the dunnest smoke of hell,
That my keen knife see not the wound it makes,
Nor heaven peep through the blanket of the dark,
To cry "Hold, hold!"

My brother, who read Freud and Shakespeare and had visions of doom, stepped in, offering to resolve the matter and end the suffering of the little ones. He explained to me that they were going to die from hunger. He said that we should spare them that fate and finish them off with dignity worthy of the bravery they had shown by withstanding the siege of Beirut.

"But how? Why not take them to the sea and release them there?"

"They're freshwater fish, but even if they weren't, the sea is littered with warships shelling us from all sides."

A plan was hatched: we pour Dettol, a concentrated antiseptic liquid, into their tank and kill them, massacre them all, in one quick blow.

Dettol is a British detergent and biocide made with pine oil that gives it its brown color. According to the Royal Society of Chemistry website, Dettol's phenol-based active ingredient, para-chloro-meta-xylenol, PCMX, binds "to proteins present on the cell membrane of bacteria, disrupting the cell membrane and allowing the contents of the cell to leak out. This allows more PCMX to enter the cell, binding further with proteins and enzymes, and effectively shutting down the cell's functions. At high concentrations of PCMX, the proteins and nucleic acids in the cell are coagulated and cease to function, leading to rapid cell death."

Dettol had a white sword plastered on the bottle, that same sword that would stop protecting us from microbes and viruses and retrieve instead its history of bloodshed during this unforgettable summer.

We poured Dettol into the tank.

The water turned white due to the emulsification of the pine oil, and the fish started floating on the surface, gasping for air, dying, one by one. With this biocide, which I would unleash on my own skin one day, we set water on fire, reproducing the effects of that vacuum bomb that incinerated the inhabitants of the Akar Building next door. Except this time, we dropped the bomb on the little ones left in our care.

By the end of that summer, the horror that was brought from the Berlin Olympics would make its way into refugee camps, buildings, households, and even fish tanks. Nothing, absolutely nothing, would be spared. Every species, every group was now a savage to the others. The monsters were everywhere, inside of us, safe within our entrails.

Why did we kill those goldfish? Was it truly a mercy killing? Perhaps we saw ourselves in the helpless creatures going round and round, moving from a bucket to a tank, not knowing what to do or where to go. Perhaps we couldn't handle seeing our own reflection in the water and we needed to blur it, to make it opaque, once and for all. The mirror was revealing something we could no longer bear to see. One final act of savagery would put all the others to rest, would spare us the restlessness of the siege, of war and death that followed us wherever we went. From fake shelters to hotel rooms, something needed to be shed, forgotten, cut off, circled around so we could carry on, immune to the events and news breaking on TV screens and radio broadcasts.

The roller skates that my parents bought me to convince me to stay in Beirut with Bahieh that summer allowed me to perform a death ritual, moving to the rhythm of the fish gasping for air in the tank and the images of gore on TV. The skates allowed me to dance around that which we cannot name, that which enters our psyche and shapes our desire. I became in the end like a camel circling the cadaver of her dead calf, of the dead fish, unable to let go, unable to accept their death. Or perhaps I'm that calf on the ground, or the orange goldfish with puffy cheeks, pretending to be dead, waiting for the right moment to break free.

9

HOTEL IVOIRE

I don't remember his name. I remember the name I gave him when he asked for mine.

He smiled as I passed him in the hallway, a special smile that I immediately recognized. The hallway was part of a large complex of lobbies and entrances, restaurants and entertainment venues. It was tucked away in the back, leading perhaps to a secret garden. It was also winding and had little traffic, especially at night, as if purposefully designed for strolling and clandestine encounters. Thinking about it today, it reminds me of that corridor at the Louisiana Museum of Modern Art outside of Copenhagen, with its glass panels and rainbow-colored lights. Crossing it feels like entering a portal to a different reality, somewhere inward, forbidden, far away.

I noticed that hallway when I was walking to meet friends at the American restaurant at the hotel. I loved that restaurant. It had long, wiry lamps that hovered over the burger plates to keep them warm. I had never seen warming lamps before. They hung from a high ceiling in a wide-open space, like divine incubators that bewildered patrons, drawing them into a spectacle that was transparent yet full of mystery. The steam and smells emanating from the burger plates rose into the incandescent bulbs like ghostly beings, unable to resist the lure of heat and light. It was as if the plates were laid on an altar, announcing the advent of a new god who shines light at the end of those tunnels and hallways where men stroll in search of special glances and secret gardens.

The men wandering the hallway close by were heat seekers as well, strange flaneurs who gave up the arcades of Paris for the comfort of American cuisine and its promise of liberation. It was, after all, 1990. The Berlin Wall had just fallen, and the first Gulf War was about to start. The whole world was entering an American hallway, marching on the *Roads to Freedom*. This freedom would crush everything in its path, even the french fries on those burger plates. It would seek us out on every shore, including here, on the West Coast of Africa and its fabled city, Abidjan.

———

Abidjan was born from the union of salt and fresh water, a union described in one of the suras of the Quran. Surrounded by the Ébrié Lagoon and connected to the Atlantic by the Vridi Canal, Abidjan was a haven of commerce and sophistication. They called it the Little Paris of Africa, and it attracted migrants and merchants from all over the world. It had a special appeal for those coming from Lebanon, the Switzerland of the Middle East. Many came on boats that hopped up and down the Mediterranean, and then veered left after Cape Spartel and the Caves of Hercules outside Tangiers. The boats cruised southward for Dakar, Conakry, and the other cities of the coast of gold and ivory.

Colonial legacies and heat-seeking men make the rules of trade and attraction.

Many of my compatriots came to this part of the world seeking fortune in business and construction. Some also came to escape wars and broken hearts and closed doors. I think of Hanan al-Shaykh's novel *The Story of Zahra*, whose main character tries yet fails to remake her life here. She left Lebanon, but Lebanon would never let go of her, not ever.

I had to leave Lebanon as well. The idea of leaving to reinvent myself would come later—for now, I needed to escape the war at its moment of climax. An army general had taken it upon himself to liberate the country from all occupiers, including those squatting in the building across from mine. I woke up one morning to the sound of bombs exploding nearby. I called the school to see if it was open, but no one picked up. My mom suggested that I should go anyway. So I went.

I remember the scene of mayhem in front of my school, with people running in all directions. Lebanon was going to be consumed by the War of Liberation (*harb al-tahrir*), a cycle of violence that would push out all those who had refused to emigrate up to that point. This was the yearlong bang that would eventually put an end to the civil war.

But like the last episode of the last season of a series that had run and run for fifteen years, many relationships would have to end in the hope of revival or rebirth in a distant future.

The rules of cohabiting with war no longer applied. When the fighting erupted in 1989, my dad had already died and my siblings and nanny had left Lebanon. My mom and I had to fend for ourselves for the first time. We were completely destitute; my brothers, who had just started working abroad, were sending some money to help us survive. We escaped to Tripoli, in the north, to stay with relatives, but after a few months there, a more long-term solution needed to be found. Calls were made and travel plans were drawn.

It was decided that my mom would go live with her sister in the U.S., and I would travel to Côte d'Ivoire to live with my older brother, who was working there. I'm not sure how this plan came about. They must have thought that I could attend a French school in Abidjan should the conflict persist. But there were surely other reasons that I couldn't understand. Beggars can't be choosers.

My mom and I returned to Beirut, packed our bags, and traveled by land through Syria to Jordan, and from there boarded planes to our respective destinations. Before leaving the house, I asked my mom if I could take the radio-cassette player she had by her bedside. A small, silver-colored player with a wide handle, it ran on either electricity or batteries. It was made by National, a Japanese brand that was part of Panasonic. This radio-cassette was her most precious object, her closest companion. And I wanted it. I had this crazy idea that I would use my headphones to transform it into a Walkman and listen to my music during the long journey. She couldn't understand why I wanted it. She felt that I was ripping away a part of her. She fought back. I insisted. She relented in the end.

My mom went to sleep every night with Umm Kulthum's songs playing on her radio. She inherited this ritual from her father, who used to stay up all night listening to the *sitt* (lady), especially the live broadcast of her concerts on the Cairo-based station Voice of the Arabs. My mom's favorite song was "Al-Atlal," which literally means "The Ruins." The song is a languorous complaint by a lover who can no longer bear the pangs of desire and separation. She pleads with her beloved to release her from her bonds and commitments. My mom loved to repeat the lines

Give me my freedom
Untie my hands,
For I have given everything
And have nothing left to give!

This was the rallying cry for women of my mom's generation, a call for liberation from the shackles of love, from matrimonial and perhaps even maternal duties. And now that my father was gone and war had broken out again, she, too, needed to be released from her bonds, to return to her father, who was living with my aunt in America, so they could all listen to Umm Kulthum together. But I had taken the radio with me and would never bring it back.

Where I come from, when husbands die, women revert to their maiden names. Losing a husband is like a divorce; even the prenuptial agreement or the contract made at the time of marriage needs to be settled after the husband's death. Come to think of it, the minute my father died, my mom shut the house down, especially the kitchen. It is as if she were saying, "I have nothing left to give." The War of Liberation was now liberating her completely from her bonds. She was returning to her clan, and I had to go join mine in Africa.

This liberation (or abandonment) is not personal and has nothing to do with love, or unconditional love for that matter. These are the laws of kinship and patriarchy, and they were the only laws that resisted the onslaught of the Lebanese Civil War.

After I said goodbye to my mother in Amman, I boarded a flight to Cairo, where I would spend the night. Having no visa to enter Egypt, I had to sleep at the airport, in a room that might as well have been a detention cell. The room's door didn't lock properly, so I was terrified that someone might break in in the middle of the night. My plane left the next day, heading to Abidjan but making stops in Kano and Lagos in Nigeria.

From Beirut to Amman by land, and from Cairo to Kano, Lagos, and Abidjan by air, my trip was already resembling other trips that I would eventually write about. Experiencing severe turbulence, the plane went up and down like a yo-yo in the sky. At one point, the lights went out midair. Panic struck. Some passengers lay on the floor and started wailing. This journey brought to mind an episode from al-Tahtawi's travelogue, *An Imam in Paris*, when a storm engulfed the ship transporting him from Alexandria to Marseille in 1826, terrifying all on board. This was the same terror that the poet al-Shanfara must have felt when he was kicked out of his tribe in sixth-century Arabia. These are the themes that I would later explore in my work.

Impossible departures and shattered bonds create a community of strangers who find each other along the way.

In Abidjan, I lived with my brother and his wife. They were newlyweds and had to practice their parenting on a teenage boy escaping war. They did it with love. It also helped that my sister-in-law's family had been in Abidjan for years, having moved there from Lebanon and nearby Guinea.

The matriarch was a woman we called *maman* ("Mom" in French). She was a tall, corpulent woman with glasses. She had a huge collection of miniature perfume bottles, *échantillons*, which she exhibited on various shelves and stands. The scents of the world had assembled in that living room, where no evil spirit dared set foot. Remembering *maman*'s bottles today makes me think of my mom's own bottle collection, ready to be deployed like a regiment of soldiers—a phalange!—whenever the need arose.

I forget in what context, but it was *maman* who declared once, "Poor Tarek, he's escaping war and has just lost his father." It took a hellish trip across land and air for me to hear this acknowledgment. I still remember her saying it in French. As a courageous Beiruti, I shrugged off war and all its downer feelings, in line with Sabri Qabbani and his "no badness no sadness" motto, which allowed my mom to survive.

But for some reason, this statement was engraved in my mind.

This matriarch in Africa had named something that would take me years to recognize.

That summer, I wasn't the only orphaned teenager escaping the Lebanese Civil War to be welcomed by *maman*'s family. Hussein was a relative whose mom had also sent him to Abidjan. He started working for his brother-in-law, selling electronics in the bustling neighborhood of Treichville. I liked Hussein a lot. I also thought he was incredibly handsome. Tall, with green eyes and perfectly drawn eyebrows, he looked like a young Val Kilmer.

It soon dawned on me that Hussein wasn't working while waiting for school to reopen in the fall. He had quit school altogether. Such is the fate of children when parents die and countries implode. This could have been my fate as well, if it weren't for family scheming and the laws of kinship, no matter how cruel and circuitous they were.

I knew a few people back home who left right after high school or halfway through college to go work in places like Treichville. When they became rich, it no longer mattered that they "didn't continue"—an awful expression that mixes shame with understanding to refer to those who dropped out of school.

Another relation that sustained me during that year in Côte d'Ivoire was with my brother's coworker, who had just finished university in Beirut. In his midtwenties, he became a friend and a confidant. He lived in the same building as my brother, and I would go up and spend a lot of time with him, discussing politics and religion, relationships and family ties. He and my brother worked for an American company that sold sewing machines in Africa. The company's offices were in the same building, and I would often help there. I learned to use the fax and telex machines. This was my first exposure to communication technology, and it was suboptimal, to say the least. I often misread and mistyped handwritten notes or failed to hit the right button to send a message. Luckily, Eric, the office manager, was always there to intervene whenever necessary.

Eric was a lovely man from Ghana who took me under his wing. He spoke fluent French and English in addition to tribal languages. He taught me how to use technology and brought me along when running errands. Soon, I became his apprentice. Eric was a Jehovah's Witness. People used to tease him about it, chiding him for not celebrating birthdays or accepting blood transfusions. I also heard that he made his kids wake up early every morning to study the Bible, even on weekends. It seems that his son complained once, but to no avail. Nothing fazed Eric. With his smile and mild manners, he managed to defuse the crudest of jokes and criticisms.

And between him and the others I met that summer, I was slowly adapting to life in Abidjan. With the conflict in Lebanon intensifying and no end in sight,

it was decided that I should start school there in the
fall, the same fall that would witness the toppling of
the Berlin Wall and the end of the Cold War.

It was a school like no other. It had a gym, an open-
air swimming pool, and a well-equipped lab. I came
from a French school in Beirut, true, but it was nothing compared to Lycée Blaise Pascal, which had been
built in 1981 outside of the city and had expanded
over the years. Most of the students were children of
expats, with a few locals, and many biracial students.
I was friends with a kid called François. His dad was
Ivorian, and his mother French. He had spent a year
in the U.S., hosted by a Mormon family in Utah.
He carried *The Book of Mormon* with him to school,
which he once showed me, explaining something
about revelation. I also became friends with a French
kid, a son of a preacher man. I think his last name was
boucles d'or (golden curls), which he had. With his curls
and droopy blue eyes, he was the true face of revelation, a cherub sent by God as proof of His beauty and
magnificence. Who would not convert upon seeing
this creature! I was beginning to understand the missionary logic in Africa. But "golden curls" was forced
to attend service every weekend with his family and
couldn't join us when we went out.

My friends came from all over. There was an
Algerian girl called Assia whose expat dad worked in

development of some sort. There was also Natasha, who was of Chinese descent but born and raised in Abidjan; her family owned the oldest Chinese restaurant in town. There was also a half-Lebanese, half-Swiss kid named Christian, with whom I became very close. His family took me in and regularly invited me to stay over at their house. There was also a half-French, half-Ivorian girl called Vanessa—I had a major crush on her. There was also a Swiss boy, Stephane, who was a bit of a troublemaker. He revealed at some point that he was in fact Armenian, or half-Swiss, half-Armenian, or something of the sort. And finally there was Yasmine, who was half-Lebanese, half-Eurasian. She explained to me that "Eurasian" meant half-European and half-Asian.

With this group of friends, I explored Abidjan. Once, we went to a restaurant called Le Vatican. One kid said that this was the most famous restaurant serving local food in town, and that George Bush (the elder) had once dined there. But the ultimate destination, the one place where everyone wanted to go on a Friday or Saturday night, was Le Grand Bleu, a famous nightclub in the Plateau district. It was named after Luc Besson's film with Jean Reno. Shot in Greece, the film was about a diver who couldn't resist the pull of the deep, eventually becoming one with the sea.

Le Grand Bleu was a perfect-sized club; it was not so big that you could get lost, and not too small, with enough room to dance and circulate. My brother came to get me from the club once and showed up while I was slow dancing. I felt like I was being picked up from school at three in the morning.

With everyone half this and half that, I started telling people that my mom was American. I, too, wanted my share of the racial mixing I was discovering in Africa. Or perhaps I was trying to strengthen my bond with my brother, who did have an American mom. I was also disowning the mother who had let go of me. What is certain is that I was trying to leave behind Lebanon and its cruel kinship laws and contracts to fully embrace the motto of our school's patron philosopher, Blaise Pascal: "The heart has its reasons that reason cannot know." But it wasn't the path to God that my heart was after, but another one, a winding one. This line from Pascal was my answer to my mom's "give me my freedom, untie my hands." Now we could both be free.

Without knowing it, my mom and I were involved in a cross-Atlantic poetic battle—Pascal vs. Umm Kulthum. Eventually this confrontation would lead me to assert my freedom and create my own community of strangers, making up names and telling stories that would get me to gardens where secrets would be revealed.

Abidjan allowed me to discover who I was, what I wanted, what I felt. I was becoming aware of myself in relation to these kids from all over the world and from all races.

One day my math teacher made a solemn declaration in front of the whole class. After I solved a math problem that no one else could, he turned to me and said, *"M El-Ariss, vous êtes trop fort pour être ici et trop faible pour être ailleurs"* (Mr. El-Ariss, you are too strong to be here and too weak to be elsewhere). He was referring to the fact that my level was somewhere between *première* and *terminale* (junior and senior high), since I had completed half of *première* in Beirut before getting interrupted by the war. But I felt he meant something else, referring to another mathematical equation that could not be solved so easily.

My math teacher's statement seems to come right out of the *Pensées* by Pascal, who was a mathematician as well. Maybe he was referring to the equation of identity, including race, sexuality, and a slew of other things. I was a Lebanese in Africa, after all, somewhere in between on the French racialist and economic scale. There were also girls I was interested in and slow dancing with at Le Grand Bleu, and hallways that called on me at night. And little did I know that I was in between war and peace, and that the distance to Beirut could collapse with the sound of any gunshot or glass breaking.

Côte d'Ivoire was hailed as the African miracle. Félix Houphouët-Boigny's rule from 1960 until his death in 1993 brought stability and prosperity to the country. This attracted people and investment, but exacerbated economic disparities. Coupled with corruption, those disparities started to simmer in state institutions—most notably the army. While I was living there, soldiers demanding better conditions mutinied. It was a class uprising within the army ranks, contesting the officers' monopoly on privileges. The mutiny of 1990 would be the preamble for political crises and wars that would plunge the country into a long spiral of violence. Nothing would be spared, not even Lycée Blaise Pascal. In 2004, a militia attacked the school and severely damaged it, forcing it to shut down for four years.

My brother and his wife lived in Marcory Résidentiel, a neighborhood adjacent to the Lebanese enclave on Rue de la Paix. It is ironic that the shop owners and inhabitants who had fled the conflict in Lebanon chose to live on "Peace Street," which was transformed overnight into a war zone when soldiers rioted in May 1990. Fighting and chaos spread across the city before things eventually settled down. This mutiny, which saw soldiers occupying the airport, was preceded by protests starting in February. Civil servants and students took to the streets decrying worsening economic conditions and demanding an end to corruption and autocratic rule. In mid-April the government decided to close all local schools for the rest of the academic year—except for the French Lycée Blaise Pascal. Our school remained open but suspended bus service due to security concerns. As the precarious situation set in, I started carpooling with kids from the neighborhood and got reaccustomed to cohabiting with war, which seemed to have followed me all the way to Africa.

The survival mechanisms I honed on the streets and beaches of Beirut were being put to the test in Abidjan. They would also be tested in New York on 9/11 and in New England, when the COVID-19 pandemic struck. I can go into a state of emergency in a wink. I know exactly what to do, what to store, where to hide. I can transform the house into a refugee camp, if need be, and into a nightclub, so we can dance the war away. I can also get water and transport and store it to withstand any siege.

Crisis mode is in my DNA.

In Abidjan, I created my enclave by the sea, transforming my room at my brother's house into a little island so that the Robinson Crusoe that I became could find solace from storms and shipwrecks. I got my provisions from the Librairie de France, a bookstore on Rue de la Paix. These books nourished me and allowed me to bear the prevailing uncertainty.

Up to that point, I had been mostly interested in poetry. I loved Baudelaire and Rimbaud and was particularly drawn to their rebellious personae and aesthetics. In Abidjan, my interest expanded to include essays, plays, and novels from the eighteenth century onward. After all, I was in *première*, and we had to prepare for the first part of the French baccalaureate, known as *anticipation*. Junior high in the French system ends with a two-part French literature exam, one written and one oral. Students must read dozens of books over the course of the year. I didn't sleep one night reading Emile Zola's *Germinal*.

The monkish impulses that would take hold later were germinating in Abidjan.

Going into my Crusoe phase allowed me to disconnect in order to reconnect again with others, with myself. The silence allowed me to read and hear voices that came from inside of me and spoke through the pages of the books I was reading. These voices converted me. But not to some religious sect preying on the vulnerable and questioning. These voices made me believe in a world that coexists with ours, just like the world of war that pursues me everywhere. Except it was a world of ghosts and fiction, and those who believed in it became my friends and interlocutors forever.

Every book became a portal to some life that I was living, that I could have lived. Marguerite Duras wrote *Un barrage contre le Pacifique* (*The Sea Wall*) and *L'amant* (*The Lover*) about her family, about how her widowed mother tried to keep them afloat in Indochina, where my school principal in Beirut fought. These novels were also about people I was meeting in Abidjan—like Géraldine, a girl I dated at school and with whom I was slow dancing at Le Grand Bleu when my brother showed up that night.

Géraldine lived with her mother and little sister in a small house with a small pool surrounded by an artificial lawn. Her mom worked for a French company, while the father was absent. But unlike Duras's family in Indochina, Géraldine and her mom took things lightly. The struggle and pain in Duras were transformed here into joie de vivre that resonated with a war survivor from Beirut and from Rue de la Paix.

Then came Nadja. She was named after the heroine in André Breton's surrealist novel of the same name. And just like Breton's relation with the real Nadja, our relation would be short yet intense. I was finally living French literature. The names in the books were materializing around me, filling rooms, breathing. The France that I was reading about in Lebanon was becoming flesh in Africa.

Other voices came calling as well. They sent me messages in bottles, promising to rescue me from the island where I had barricaded myself with Zola, Duras, and Voltaire. They had come to take me to other shores where I would be free, completely free.

But I eventually realized that there are no books on those other shores, and no ghosts either. Those shores were across the westerly sea, the sea of darkness, where the monstrous phoenix carries her prey, never to bring them back. It's the same sea that my mom had crossed to reunite with her family, leaving me behind so I could forge my own.

The voices kept calling. They came from every-where. They were entering my body. Speaking in my head, with my voice. I became like Faust in Goethe's play when he declares: "Two souls live in me. Alas, irreconcilable to one another." These two souls, this division, that split on the mathematical scale that was announced in class, put me in the middle of a struggle between the libertine and the monk. This struggle that is life, at its end, could never be resolved without some grand event like war and displacement, or, as in Goethe's play, without the advent of the devil.

When I understood *Faust*, I, too, made a deal with the devil on that island of mine, calling for salvation while playing Alpha Blondy, Prince, and Grace Jones songs on my mother's radio-cassette.

I was saved by a colonial bookstore on Rue de la Paix, only to be doomed by a pact with a French-speaking Mephisto. This devil was going to transport me to the birthplace of freedom and fries, at the end of a long, winding hallway.

The winding hallways of Hotel Ivoire were built by the Israeli architect and developer Moshe Mayer. It is said that the Côte d'Ivoire's president Houphouët-Boigny met Mayer on a visit to Monrovia, Liberia, in 1960. Houphouët fell in love with Hotel Ducor, a mod-ernist gem overlooking the Atlantic that Mayer had built, so he asked him to build a nicer, bigger one in Abidjan. Mayer commissioned his compatriots Heinz Fenchel and Thomas Leitersdorf to design the complex, which was completed in stages between 1963 and 1970.

Hotel Ivoire would rise from the Ébrié Lagoon as the work of a jinni who had to outdo himself to impress his new master. With its pools and casino, ice-skating rink and movie theater, this marvelous complex would rival the cathedral built on the other side of the lagoon. The hotel would pluck the stars from the sky, one by one, and bring them to perform in its concert hall and to adorn its lobbies and restaurants. Michael Jackson and Mohammed Ali stayed at the hotel. And Stevie Wonder performed there as well; Jacques, a kid in my class, attended the concert and told us all about it.

The hotel's luster would gradually fade. War and crises took a toll on this crown jewel. Parts of it would be turned into a military headquarters due to its tower's strategic overlook on the city. In this way, it would share the fate of Beirut's hotels, where snipers nestled in their high floors and graffiti-ridden rooms during Lebanon's civil war. And just like the hotels back home, Hotel Ivoire would eventually close, awaiting reconstruction. And who better than a Lebanese to undertake this project?

Architect Pierre Fakhoury, an Ivorian of Lebanese descent, was hired to renovate the hotel in 2009, and it reopened two years later. Built by an Israeli and brought back by a Lebanese, the hotel was destined to play out some of the conflicts in the Middle East, lured to Abidjan by fortune of all kinds. But something about Hotel Ivoire was about a desire that could not be fulfilled in our region. Ultimately, Lebanese and Israelis had to come to Africa to overcome their kinship rules and take part in a nation-building and rebuilding project. What they built brought about modernity and liberation, burgers and bowling alleys, and hallways that meander and lead to inner gardens where secrets and bodies are exposed.

It was a rainy night. My brother was away on one of his business trips. My sister-in-law had gone to stay with her parents. I was by myself in the apartment. I decided to take a taxi to Hotel Ivoire in search of those strolling in the winding hallways. I started walking, looking, not sure what I was going to find. I passed a beautiful woman in traditional wrapper clothing, or *pagne*. She looked at me and asked: "Are you staying at the hotel?" I politely said no and walked away.

Strolling some more, a man appeared at the end of the hallway. He was in his late thirties, tall, not particularly handsome, French. He turned to me and smiled. My heart started racing. I pursued him. I went to him and asked, "Are you staying at the hotel?" He said yes. "What is your name?" He told me and then asked for mine. "Jean," I answered.

Where did "Jean" come from? And how did he muster the courage to go strolling in these hallways at night? Maybe I was anticipating Jean Genet and Edmund White, Genet's biographer, both of whose works I would later discover. I was also anticipating the most common name for the beloved in Arabic novels set in Europe.

While in English Jean is a woman's name, in French Jean is that of a man. Something about this name and its cross-gendered derivatives captures a tale of unspoken love, a passionate encounter that takes hold of one's mind, life, being. Between the masculine and feminine "Jean," the floodgates of literature were opening. This is what I would later call *Trials of Arab Modernity*.

The bold and resourceful Jean would be my hero from that moment on. He had plans and acted upon them with great determination. Characters were no longer ghostly figures who lived in books and fantasies. They were now actors on the stage of life and war, which stretched from the beaches of Beirut to Abidjan's lagoons.

I was learning to accept the union between the world of fiction and my reality, between the world of ghosts and that of living beings who seek heat and flesh for pleasure and nourishment.

————

I was never into sci-fi. Intimate bonds between humans and machines or strange creatures never appealed to me. Not until I got infected with the Cayor worm, a kind of blowfly that's also known as the tumbu fly. Its scientific name is *Cordylobia anthropophaga*, a reference to its "human-eating" quality. When researching this tropical-climate fly that starts its life as a worm, I realized that American medical sources had little to say about this condition compared to their European counterparts, especially the French and the Belgians, who had spent years colonizing and studying Africa.

Should a tumbu fly larva come into contact with human skin, it clings to it, pokes it, and starts growing in the epidermal cavities. What first looks like a pimple ends up becoming within a week or so a little worm that strolls through one's flesh like something in a scene from *Alien*.

The womb that Crusoe had created on his desert island was now in my forearm, birthing a strange creature that turned my body into a hallway for a flesh-eating flaneur.

To encourage the Cayor worm to leave its newfound home, an entire seduction scene has to be staged. Some American doctors suggest putting a piece of bacon on the lesion, asserting that the worm will stick to it and thus be more easily discarded. Other treatments involve Vaseline, which cuts off the air that the worm needs to grow.

I used red palm oil. Eric, the company's office manager and Cayor worm midwife extraordinaire, told me that the oil's pungent smell would lure the worm to the surface. He got me the oil and the antibiotics to go with it. All I had to do was drizzle the oil over the orifice to get the creature out.

Indeed, the worm was curious and stuck its head out multiple times, but never left its hole. This reminds me of how my mom describes my birth: "You were happy inside and didn't want to leave. You almost killed me." The worm almost killed me from pain as it was strolling in the hallway under my skin. While my mom was surrounded by doctors, including my father, who would finally extract me with forceps, I was by myself at home, calling Eric for instructions. In and out and in and out until it stopped moving. The baby beast was dead. Perhaps it was not ready to face this evil world. Either that or it overdosed on the red palm oil that I kept pouring in and around the orifice, hoping to lure it out.

The worm was stuck halfway. I could see its head, while the body remained inside. I went to the sink and squeezed it out of its subdermal cavity. My arm was so swollen that it looked like a mountain of pus. I took antibiotics and healed soon after.

The worm burrowing under my skin reminds me of those men strolling up and down hallways late at night. Is this what the devil understood when I asked for someone to love? The pact seems to have gone terribly wrong. Or perhaps this was part of the bargain: for every person "Jean" meets I would have an alien creature enter my body and devour my flesh. This is the kind of bargain the Marquis de Sade wrote about in the eighteenth century, or that people had to contend with in the age of AIDS. This impossible bargain would shape my desire and lure strange and tiny creatures to flesh, oils, and pheromones.

But there is another explanation. The Cayor worm that started growing in my forearm died for its desire. It died a martyr's death, as it would never compromise or make concessions. From it I learned that I, too, would desire to the death. Pushing it out at the end felt like I was pushing myself out of my own body, in a final act of liberation—a small death.

The liberation war that consumed Lebanon that year and severed my ties to my mom made my skin produce alien beings that come out of twisted imagination and true desire. The "poor Tarek" who had lost his parents and was escaping war was giving birth to himself in Africa. I felt like Tolstoy's Anna Karenina, whom they sent away to give birth to her love child with Count Vronsky. It was a birthing through war but also through literature.

The quest for love will always be etched on my body, threatening it with invasion by alien creatures who will come to me as I strike out on my own in

search of my community of strangers. This is the price
of desire, perhaps, the price of believing in those ghosts
that will haunt and prevent me from sleeping at night.
By taking my mom's radio-cassette, I replaced the
voice of Umm Kulthum with the voice of Mephisto
from Goethe's *Faust*. It was speaking to me at night,
instructing me to stroll in winding hallways near and
far, and demanding that I pay with my flesh so that I
could be free.

10

THUGS

He wanted my notebook. The cover was deep green and was stamped with my university logo. It had everything. Notes from class, drawings, phone numbers. Everything was there, in the main text, and sprawling into the margin, going deep into the little holes that the metal spiral penetrates and binds.

In one of the drawings, there is a Medusa-like figure. The hair is long and snakes from the skull into the air, vertically, obliquely, in all directions. The figure is slim, undulating, resembling a pantomime, or a deus ex machina descending from the top of the page to subvert the outcome of a play or an epic.

I had terrible handwriting and used abbreviations for recurrent terms, with the Greek letter Φ (phi) standing for "philosophy," and Ψ (psi) for "psychology." An *ion* following a *t* at the end of words was represented by a small circle with a dash beneath. These notes and scribbles revealed a new sign system, a hieroglyph that gave shape to words and sounds that were legible only to me. It was my language, my writing, yet he wanted it and I couldn't say no.

I used to carry my books and notebooks without a strap or a bag. I would stack them together, holding them tight in my small hand while they kept falling from all sides. What mattered was that the cover of my little stack that I carried around town had the American University of Beirut (AUB) inscription clearly visible, for all to see. This stamp of belonging made me feel safe, no matter what I was carrying or how I was carrying myself.

But there was something else about the looseness of these books and notebooks in my hand that was not only about safety and belonging. There was something about their looseness that reflected the meandering scribbles and anagrams on the inside. Something about this disorder, this vulnerability, needed to be shown as well.

He wanted my notebook. Perhaps he wanted to understand the chaos that I held within me and that held me together.

I used to walk to the university from our house in Sanayeh. When it rained, I would tuck my stack underneath my heavy leather jacket and close the zipper as if I were protecting a naked child, a cherub made of salt or sugar. I embraced my books and notebooks; I held them close to my heart. As they rubbed against my abdomen, the iron tips of the spiral binding would get caught in my wool sweaters, pulling at their threads. The metal spiral would get bent and twisted every time the notebook fell to the floor, or when I accidentally sat on it in the packed cafeteria. At the end, the spiral lost its linear circularity and became crooked, making it harder to turn the page.

So when he asked for my notebook, I felt that he was asking to penetrate my crookedness, crack my code, uncover my secret.

He had a rectangular face and a black beard that descended to his chin and went back up to his hairline. He was in his midthirties and wore mostly black. He was always on the go, always talking to someone, floating on campus, making sure that all was under control.

When he showed up to class, he sat quietly in the back and said little if anything at all. It was as if he were daydreaming, or solving a problem that required a different kind of logic. He was there to protect us, like a bodyguard, or to protect us from ourselves, to make sure that no ill was ever uttered or thought, that no devil could ever find its way into our heads and speak through us.

Eventually, I learned that he was the student leader of one of the main political factions in Lebanon, a faction with a powerful militia and a bloody history. For

now, he was in my class, majoring in philosophy, and
going on his tenth or fifteenth year of college.

He came to me before the exam and asked for my
notebook. I was in the library, which was packed with
students studying during finals season. It was winter-
time and everyone had big coats and heavy sweaters
spread all over the long tables. He entered the room,
walked up to me, and asked for my notebook. I was
terrified. What did I do? What am I being accused of?
What evidence was he going to find in this book of
riddles? All eyes were on us.

He said he needed it for one day only. He wanted
to copy it and promised to return it unharmed. But
why me? Doesn't he realize that all the blabber I utter
in class was for attention only? Doesn't he know that
just like him, I, too, was an intruder to philosophy? I
should have kept my mouth shut. How was I going to
study without my constellation of signs and anagrams?
How was I going to find my way without this astrolabe
to guide me across the deserts and oceans of the mind?

I had to give it to him. I couldn't say no. I didn't
sleep that night. His militia had kidnapped my brother
during the war. They cut him off while he was driving and abducted him right by our house. They took
him to a dungeon in the basement of a building,
interrogated him, and beat him up before eventually
releasing him. It was the longest day of our lives.

He returned the notebook. I'm not sure what information he got from it or how useful it was for studying

for an exam that he had failed repeatedly. Finally, he exhausted the number of times that one can take and fail a course, leading our department chair to have a talk with him, to convince him to drop the major, to leave philosophy alone. This meant that he was going to be expelled from the university and lose his thug status. He made threats, but the chair stood his ground.

In the end, I stopped seeing him on campus. His party must have replaced him with someone else, a little bit younger perhaps, a little less conspicuous, for sure. It was the early nineties, after all, and the war that had supposedly ended needed new faces and masks to continue.

The war was over Just like that. It took the fall of the Berlin Wall and of the Soviet Union and Saddam Hussein's invasion of Kuwait for a Pax Americana to emerge in the region and around the globe. I remember when the Gulf War started. I was back from Côte d'Ivoire and finishing my last year of high school in Beirut. When the Americans and their allies launched their assault on the Iraqi forces in Kuwait in February 1991, I was in math class. The teacher stopped the lecture to listen to the news on the small radio that he had brought along. The reporter was announcing a resounding Iraqi victory.

An Arab leader sending Scud missiles on Israel and destroying a sprawling allied army led by the U.S.

was worth interrupting class for that day. Everyone cheered except for one kid, a cynic, a wise guy, a party pooper. He looked at everyone with disdain and said that the news was false and that what was being hailed as a victory was nothing but a crushing defeat. He was right.

The war was over. Roadblocks were removed and borders dividing cities and regions dismantled. People from West Beirut could now get in their car and drive to the East, discover a country that was theirs but that they hadn't seen before. And people from the East could now attend AUB or go to the airport on the west side without fearing abduction or sniper fire. We were finally free to go everywhere and do everything and come up with our own sign systems. In a bizarre way, the war of liberation that was the big bang that ended the Lebanese Civil War seemed to have fulfilled its promise.

We were free at last. No bombs or fake shelters or ID cards stating our sects. There was a euphoria in the air, a thirst to reunite, to see each other for who we were, to shun politics and the ideologies that led us to ruin. We were entering the decade of love. A new stage was being built and everyone wanted to be on it, practicing new roles, styles, and desires.

The war was over, but the smell of garbage and gunfire was still in our nostrils. We needed to be pinched, slapped, convinced that the nightmare that had been our reality for the last fifteen years was now truly—truly—over. The nostalgia for the war started immediately with its end. So when a friend from the East told me once that she grew up thinking that West Beirut was a jungle inhabited by beasts, I wasn't surprised at all. In fact, I, too, thought that our part of the city was a bit of a jungle, with rampant abductions and killings and chaotic lines at bakeries and gas stations, and fights breaking out on a whim. But despite it all, when we used to cross back from East to West Beirut during the war and were greeted by the smell of garbage piling up underneath the Barbir Bridge, my father used to breathe a sigh of relief. This was the smell of home.

We cherished our jungle life. We learned how to extract from its smells and potholes a sense of safety that relieved us once we crossed that bridge. We must have been savages, but we were savages who felt pride in their state of nature. We were real, authentic, uncompromising, impervious to artifice. We were the true Beirutis, the salt of this city that sediments on the windows and cars parked by the seafront, and that lingers on the skin after washing or bathing. We lived in the jungle and could act like thugs and beasts, but also knew the ways of the world. Nothing impressed us or made us feel lacking, no matter the garbage and surrounding chaos. We were like those shameless Cyclopes in the *Odyssey* that belonged to a different era, that had a special kind of logic, never questioning the cruelty of their belonging to those caves and volcanic islands.

But with the war's end, a big broom was going to sweep away all the garbage and smells that piled up on the streets and deep within our nostrils. It was also threatening to sweep away our pride, our steadfastness, our memories. A company called Solidere moved into the bombed-out city center with bulldozers to demolish, rebuild, sanitize. Artists and intellectuals cried out: What about our memory, our pain, our sacrifices? Those bombed-out buildings were the mirror that was going to prevent us from forgetting the war, from killing each other once again! How could they erase them so brutally, so quickly? How can we let go?

But for the war to be truly over, something about our beastliness needed to be wiped out as well, demolished in a public spectacle in which we were both victims and spectators.

It all started out with the killing of the dogs. As the bulldozers moved downtown, rumors of wild dogs abducting babies from their cribs began to circulate. The temple of war was being desecrated, and the beast master ordered his devils to punish the city dwellers by devouring their firstborn.

These dogs that inhabited the abandoned city center emerged like the rats in Camus's *Plague*, spewing terror from the belly of the earth. Security forces were mobilized. Hunting parties went out every night with rifles and pickup trucks, killing and piling up the bodies of the wild beasts. These hunting parties remind me of those angry townsmen you see in the movies, chasing down werewolves with oil lamps and silver bullets.

I saw one of those trucks coming out of the city center one morning. I distinctly remember the limbs of the bloodied cadavers dangling from the back.

The war was over, and the dogs of Beirut's city center needed to be killed, punished for the crime of war, for which no leader was ever held accountable. With time, these dogs entered our psyche, appearing in Hoda Barakat's novel *The Tiller of Waters*. Barakat tells the story of a man who escapes war by moving into his father's bombed-out shop in the city center. There, he befriends a wild dog and starts a relationship with a woman who comes out of the surrounding neighborhoods and of his imagination. Barakat tells the story of the dogs to mourn them, to rehabilitate them for a crime that stuck to them by virtue of who they were and where they lived. The dogs, for Barakat, are present at the beginning of love, softening and forging the human that needed to escape the war to love again.

But for now, the time was for a different kind of love that demanded animal sacrifice, according to the ancient rituals of our religions.

At university, my childhood friend began dating a girl whose family was not only from another religion but belonged to a political party that had led the charge against the people in the western enclave. The two fell in love, like Romeo and Juliet. Perhaps it was an exotic love, a reverse demonization leading to a consuming passion that said, I missed you for fifteen years with every kiss, with every sigh.

She was his first girlfriend. He was tall and handsome, with hazel eyes and silky brown hair that he combed to the side. He was a swimmer and competed in university games in the U.S. and elsewhere. He was lighthearted and had a dry sense of humor. She was full of life, with an endemic energy that awakened the dead. There is an expression for that in Arabic: *nighsheh.*

I quickly became the companion of and go-between for my friend and his first love. I kept that love flowing through food and excursions, vicariously taking part in their amorous reunification of Beirut. The three of us became inseparable. We would wait for each other to finish our classes and then hop in the car and go explore this newly opened country. We'd go up to the mountains, to the south, to the north. And with my mom being away most of the time, either traveling or visiting with friends, our house became the nest of this new relationship.

I used to cook for them. Their favorite dish was pizza. I would buy the dough from the nearby bakery and add to it tomato sauce, olives, canned mushrooms, and layers of cheese. They loved my pizza, although the dough was always half-baked. I was never a good baker. With pizza, I had to make a choice between thoroughly cooking the dough or burning the cheese on top. It never occurred to me that I should perhaps cook the dough first or make it a bit thinner before adding the toppings and placing it in the oven. Something about baking and the laws of chemistry escaped me.

The dough I used for pizza was the same dough I used for fishing when I was a child. And though I never managed to bake it properly, my new fish friends, just like the ones who came to me as a child, liked it and kept coming for more.

By the end of our first semester at AUB, we had done so little studying and preparing—other than pizza—that he failed two classes, she failed one, and I barely, and I mean barely, passed that term. He lost his scholarship. I remember his parents yelling at him when they learned the news. They knew something was wrong. It must be a girl distracting him. It *was* a girl, and his mom went to war against her. She found out that this girl was from the other side.

Suddenly, the war erupted again in his household, on the phone, with fights in the parking lot.

One day, his mom called me and asked me to bring her—that "harlot" who was destroying her son's life. She wanted me to be the henchman, the thug from West Beirut who drags people from their homes and neighborhoods in front of their families and fellow students. She wanted me to bring her to interrogation so she could be roughed up, tortured, killed in some basement. Didn't his mom realize that the war was over, that we can't be thugs anymore? Didn't she know that I, too, was complicit in this game of love that was ruining her son's career?

She wanted me to bring her, and I couldn't say no.

One day, a summit was called. It was like those meetings that I had seen on TV, where Israelis and Palestinians, or Soviets and Americans would come together and engage in difficult negotiations. These meetings always started with accusations ranging from terrorism to sabotage to imperialism.

I ended up bringing her. She and I went to his house in the afternoon. He wasn't there. His mom started:

"My son is young, he has his career ahead of him, there is plenty of time for relationships later in life. What about your parents, do they approve of this relationship? Leave my son alone!"

"Your son is failing because of you. You've crushed him, erased his personality. He's running away from the house, from you!"

It went on like this for a portion of that afternoon. The grievances and accusations flew like bombs and bullets between the two sides, between East and West Beirut. His father was there too. He was a general in the security services. Neither he nor I uttered a word.

———

I started college not knowing what I wanted to major in. The family thought biology or premed would be the path forward. Since my brothers and sister went on to different careers, I was expected to take over the family business. But I was not good at biology or chemistry or baking for that matter. All the terms that refer to cells and membranes were not poetic enough for me. Something about the constitution of the body, which I would later write about, evaded me as a teenager and son of a doctor. I ended up passing my French baccalaureate with a science focus because I was good at math and physics. But my heart was in poetry, history, and the arts.

My mom was open to a business administration major because she thought I would at least make money, and we needed money, especially after my father died in 1987. But after one semester taking science and economics courses, I realized that neither of these fields interested me. I had big questions to answer and crises to resolve. I started taking courses in the humanities and ended up majoring in philosophy. I never looked back.

The philosophy department at AUB had a long and distinguished history, with luminaries like Sadiq Jalal al-Azm, who studied and taught there in the sixties. Eventually he was accused of apostasy and of fomenting sectarian tensions, and of anti-Americanism because of his Marxist views. He was the cousin of my aunt's husband, who was Syrian as well, and whose family escaped the commando operation during the Israeli invasion of Lebanon in 1982. When it came time for me to apply to graduate schools in the U.S., my mom took me to Damascus to ask him for advice. I had read his work before, especially his defense of Salman Rushdie against the fatwa leveled against him, and his critique of Edward Said's thesis in *Orientalism*.

We visited al-Azm in his house in the Malki neighborhood of Damascus. When he opened the door, I discovered a giant of a man in Birkenstocks and tennis shorts and thick-rimmed glasses. He was kind and humble, inquiring about my interests and offering advice about some of the programs that I should consider. I asked him about his experience teaching philosophy at the University of Damascus, and whether he was free to say whatever he wanted. He said that there were sacred cows that one needed to avoid. He said it with a sense of resignation, but one that would transform into outright rebellion with the start of the uprising in Syria in 2011. I would later run into him in Berlin and in the U.S. and fondly recollect our first encounter.

When I started my studies in the philosophy department at AUB, both the civil war and the Cold War were over. Politics was the last thing on people's minds. In fact, what drew me to the department were the mild manners of the chair, who welcomed me and offered me a home. He taught courses on ethics and political philosophy, introducing me to the works of Kant and Rawls, Nozick and Mill. I also took courses with an Oxford-trained philosopher who taught logic and Greek philosophy. Another professor who had studied at Cornell taught epistemology, philosophy of science, and metaphysics. There was also a phenomenologist on the faculty; in her classes, I discovered Husserl, Bergson, Schutz, and the hermeneutical tradition. The department offered a mix of analytic and continental philosophy, this is in addition to other classes across campus focusing on interdisciplinary approaches to philosophy, literature, and art.

One of the formative classes I took was on existentialism. We read Sartre, Camus, Kierkegaard, Schopenhauer, Heidegger, Nietzsche, and Dostoevsky, whom I already loved. I had been reading Russian literature on my own. I once read Tolstoy's *War and Peace* in one sitting. I didn't sleep or eat or shower for twenty-four hours. Even when I had to go to the bathroom, I took the novel with me. And I had no problem remembering all the names and nicknames and titles that Tolstoy threw at his reader.

I had been reading all this in French and English translations, but I wanted to read them in Russian. I wanted to immerse myself in the phonetic world of these characters, who were struggling just as I was to understand their place in the world. I wanted to read the Grand Inquisitor telling Alyosha in Dostoevsky's *The Brothers Karamazov*, "But finally the foolish children will understand that although they are rebels, they are feeble rebels, who cannot endure their own rebellion." I wanted to hear it in Russian, to understand something about the rebellion that was brewing in me, to predict how far it might go and for how long.

One day, I went to the Russian cultural center by my old school in Verdun. It was 1993 and Yeltsin was in power. I met the teacher, who was Lebanese. He had thick, black-rimmed glasses, and jet-black, almost spiky hair that was drenched in brilliantine. He looked exactly like Brezhnev or one of those cadres of the Soviet politburo. The center had just changed its name from the "Soviet" to the "Russian" cultural center. When a cheeky student asked our teacher what he thought of Yeltsin, he said: "He gives me nightmares!"

In class, the Russian language teacher gave us examples from professions like that of the *inzhener* (engineer) and *fizik* (physicist), but nothing from literature. Nothing from Tolstoy or Dostoevsky, let alone Gogol or Turgenev. Nothing. I soon realized that the kids in class were planning to go work in Russia or study engineering or the like. Sensing my frustration, a student turned to me and said: "What are you doing here?" I left the class and never came back.

What was I looking for in that Russian class? Yes, it was great to learn about the *myakyi znak*, but I was looking for interlocutors, people who recognized if not shared my desire. It soon became clear to me that my attraction to philosophy and literature was not for the pure love of ideas and languages. I was looking for a lived experience and rebelled when I didn't find it. I was looking for heroic figures inside and outside the text. I wanted this heroism to rub off on me and pull at the thread of my wool sweaters. I was craving figures to crack my shell and launch me into a world of action. I was seeking characters who went on the stage of postwar Beirut to perform their latest moves, wearing their most outrageous outfits. I wanted to live philosophy and challenge morality and norms. The pain of the existentialists and of my war years had to be transformed into a force that knows no master. I wanted to practice the rebellion that Camus wrote about in *The Rebel*, scanning the canon of literature and philosophy for the voices and acts of contestation.

I was looking for these thug-like characters in teachers and students, and I was determined to find them.

When she told me that her name in Armenian meant "she-devil," I fell in love with her then and there. For me, she was the lady version of that rebellious archangel in Milton's *Paradise Lost*. She looked like Pierrot from the commedia dell'arte and a Kabuki actor. She wore thick white foundation, silver eyeshadow, and red lipstick. Her white hair was always made up, and her glasses magnified a pair of piercing brown eyes sparkling with intelligence. She was a graduate of the philosophy department at AUB and eventually got her doctorate in the Soviet Union. She studied art as well and was herself a painter. She made snide comments that rivaled those of the Dowager Countess in *Downton Abbey*.

This she-devil was a freak among her peers and took pride in being one. She looked at me one day and said, "I'm a weirdo magnet, don't you think?" She was the priestess of the cult to which I was finally going to belong, a cult of little thugs and devils and lost souls and wanderers that were neither from East nor West Beirut but transcended their division.

Years later, when she visited me in New York, she got me a lapis lazuli candleholder that looked like the Kaaba. I was the weirdo circling around the magnet that holds the meteorite, the sacred stone that fell from the heavens and that almost wiped us out in that missile strike on our building in 1982.

Her course on the philosophy of art was a magnet for the weirdos that would become my new friends and girlfriends and partners in crime. She brought in Kafka with Van Gogh with Freud's *Interpretation of Dreams*. She asked us to feel and experience what we were reading and seeing. She wanted us to freely associate, to embark on the wings of writing with no censor, no holding back, no intrusion. From her I learned that while philosophy provided the language to confront crises and make sense of them, it was literature and art that allowed them to live, to go on the stage that was opening after the end of the Lebanese Civil War. She told me once that great art would come out of the war experience. And great art did indeed come out.

While most of the people I met at college were getting ready to benefit from Lebanon's reconstruction industry, the weirdos who flocked to the she-devil were looking to stare down the abyss that was opening within them. We were like those kids who went through Zoom teaching during the COVID-19 pandemic, except ours lasted for fifteen years. We were unsocialized or socialized in such ways that we could not settle for theories or disciplines or conventions. We had become beastly, wilder than those dogs that came out of the city's belly. We were the cynics (dogs) and existentialists and militiamen combined. This is what Derrida would call *les voyous* (thugs). We were watching *Hair, Jesus Christ Superstar,* and Almodóvar films and listening to the Seattle bands. It was among this motley crew of questioning misfits and outrageous rebels that I had found my kin, what Baudelaire once called *mon semblable, mon frère* (my alias, my twin).

His nom de guerre was Razan. In Arabic, Razan refers to rationality and reason. Literally it means "the grounded one." But for him, Razan, which is a girl's name, was more of a state of being, a sound, an elongation mimicking his long body and hair, curling up in the Beirut sun. He sang in a rock band, channeling the greats, such as Freddie Mercury, Kurt Cobain, and Robert Plant. Razan loved being on stage and had innate confidence in his power to seduce, argue, and win. He became a philosophy major and joined the cult of the weirdo magnet. The Medusa drawing in my notebook was of him.

Razan and I had gone to the same high school but weren't close back then. It was only when we met again at AUB that we both realized that we had been looking for each other, that we had already met in a previous life of mischief. We were like two witches who were going to join forces to make unbreakable spells. Our first conversation was about Marquis de Sade's *Philosophy in the Bedroom*, one of the most vehement revolutionary texts in existence, but one disguised as a pornographic novel from the eighteenth century. Razan realized that behind that goody-goody Beiruti cloak was a sick and twisted mind. Maybe he sensed a flair for debauchery waiting to pop from beneath those oversized clothes, hand-me downs from my brothers. Something was eager to break free from beneath my thinning curly hair, which was kept together with a styling gel that left blue streaks on the line where the scalp and the forehead meet, and by the ear, and down toward my neck.

The code that I was hiding in my notebook's anagrams and scribbles was finally going to be uncovered, and it was Razan who was going to push it out into the open.

Razan and I started taking our classes together, advocating theories and challenging teachers, and leaving the classroom only to continue our discussions for hours later, till we fell asleep. We used to hang out on the green oval—a patch of greenery on the AUB campus that became our headquarters. There we opened a philosophy clinic to solve crises of faith and sex and everything in between. I remember a girl came to us because she was debating losing her virginity with her boyfriend, and a pious guy who felt his faith was shaken after reading Nietzsche. We argued with religious fundamentalists and contested their interpretations of holy texts by using arguments from analytic philosophy

The she-devil's students were practicing the Socratic mantra: corrupting the youth at AUB. We should have been stoned or made to drink poison like Socrates, or at least locked up in some dungeon like the incomparable Marquis de Sade or some subversive character from West Beirut. But we were practicing philosophy out loud, and there was no turning back.

Once, Razan and I French-kissed in the seminar on Plato. Gently, the professor said: "Could you please kiss outside of my class?" We answered that it is normal for two men to kiss in a class on Greek philosophy, and that, after all, he should consider this an illustration of Plato's *Symposium*. He rolled his eyes.

We also used to kiss on the green oval as a public performance. We were not lovers or interested in each other romantically. We were purposefully seeking to violate public morality, to shock, tease, play. It was a great coming out, but not as any fixed identity or sexual orientation, because we were rebellious against those as well. It was a thug desire, informed by philosophy and orchestrated by rituals of circling around the green oval and a lapis lazuli cube offered by the high priestess of our new cult.

While I was still worried about who saw or said what, Razan was shameless, wearing his desire on his sleeve. He had tattoos before they were even fashionable. His notebook was his body, inscribing it with riddles and signs for all to see. Razan was writing his own character, and that he did with great method and attention. With time, he pushed me to assert myself. I learned that people react to our demeanor, to what we project, and to the persona we choose for the stage. If we feel shame and insecurity, people see it and rub it in. But if we walk and act with confidence, they recognize it and treat us accordingly and never single us out in a library study room to take our notebook away. We showed people what was right, what could be done, by how we did it, by how we carried ourselves and our notebooks. We had to invent our own sign system and impose it on the world rather than

wait for acknowledgment and recognition. Performing gender and sexuality, topics that I would discover
later in the works of Judith Butler and others when
I moved to the U.S., started on the stage that Razan
and I were forging at AUB.

My mom didn't like Razan. It was a clash of styles,
mostly. My mom was the Elizabeth Taylor type, glam-
orous and reserved like her in *Cleopatra*. Razan was a
vulgar and trashy seductress like the Egyptian actress
Nadia al-Gindi, or a character from Almodóvar's *Law
of Desire* or John Waters's *Pink Flamingos*. My mom
would not let her sentiment be unknown either. She
repeatedly told me that I shouldn't hang out with him,
that he was a loser, soiling our good name, destroying my career. She also vehemently abhorred his long,
curly hair. She would give him dirty looks every time
he came over.

Razan understood my mom's disdain and gave it
back tenfold. I, of course, was stuck in the middle,
watching a ping-pong game between two powerful and determined queens. The encounter was akin
to the summit I had attended with my friend's girlfriend and his mom. The salvos in my case were facial
expressions of disgust, dishonor, disappointment. But
the mother that brought Razan and me together was
a she-devil who taught philosophy as the art of rebellion in thought and action.

Razan and I became obsessed with *Bamba Kashar*,
an Egyptian movie about a courtesan who gets her

heart broken and decides to live a depraved life, taking revenge on love. Nadia al-Gindi, who played Bamba, became, along with Sade's Dolmoncé and Dostoevsky's Ivan Karamazov, the heroic figures that we modeled our desires and philosophy on. Except our broken heart was not from a treacherous lover who took advantage of us at a vulnerable age, or a god who abandoned his children when they disobeyed his commands. Our heart had been broken a long time ago and was deprived of even the fake shelters of the Lebanese Civil War.

In the world that Razan and I inhabited, there was no redemption or consolation for our broken hearts. We already understood if not anticipated what Lacan would eventually say about love and desire, that it can never be fulfilled, let alone recognized. So we decided to avenge our human condition, the condition of the weirdos and misfits and wanderers circling around a lapis lazuli cube, giving up on redemption altogether. We entered philosophy to leak its secrets, to learn how to fight fire with fire, to discover those rebels who are our kin, from Sade to the she-devil who taught and inspired us.

It was time for action.

Having exhausted the stock of weirdos hovering around the green oval, Razan and I sought other pastures. It became a game for us, with masks and role-play and accompanying soundtracks. We moved to the Corniche—the seacoast lining AUB—and Ramlet al-Baida. We went out at night, looking to feed on those who were looking to be fed upon, to be turned into the vampires that Razan and I had become, always had been. We had been watching *Bram Stoker's Dracula* and *Interview with the Vampire* and were looking to practice what we were consuming and what was consuming us. We would drive down to the coast and partake in the procession of heat seekers, performing their nightly pilgrimage by the beach where Job had once healed after a sadistic experiment that saw his flock perish and his skin break.

Once, Razan and I were driving along the coast and spotted a potential heat seeker in a car next to us. After exchanging a few glances, we cut him off with our car, as if to force him to stop. It was like those scenes from the movies when thugs cut someone off and force them to stop to abduct them or steal their car. Except we just wanted to talk, perform, feed.

After a conversation by the beach, we decided to go indoors for the real party. I remember his eyes and round glasses, which looked like psychedelic lollipops. This must have inspired Razan to take over the DJing that night, playing "Trust in Me" from *The Jungle Book* soundtrack. As the music played, we both proceeded to perform a ritual that terrorized and titillated the poor guy. We were playing Kaa to an amused and incredulous Mowgli, singing to him while moving like possessed snakes:

Trust in me, just in me,
Shut your eyes and trust in me

At the end, Razan returned to the music deck and played another song from the same soundtrack. "We're your friends, we're your friends!"

The kids from the jungle that was West Beirut had lofty ambitions in vice and corruption but were now wrapping themselves around their victims' bodies like giant snakes that sang and shivered. We were mocking romance and true love, petty passions that had no room in our philosophy manual. We took seriously the "corruption of the youth" as the ultimate lesson of philosophy, from Socrates to Kaa in *The Jungle Book*. We insisted on practicing this lesson on the green oval, on the Corniche, and in the bedroom. We were determined to turn Job's suffering and absolution at Ramlet al-Baida into a shattering force that would engulf the city and devour its dwellers. Job was awakening like Chronos on the coast of Beirut, or like a giant python from a Disney film.

Razan and I sheltered our hearts, casting away the narrative of love and romance that fell short of the lofty ideals of philosophy we practiced during our college days. We were soldiers of philosophy, thugs from West Beirut, insisting on the heroic life, the authentic life that we had convinced ourselves of leading.

Desire was incompatible with love and relationships. Freud said it as well. To be true to one's desire is to pursue human nature to its windiest hallways and darkest dungeons, to the end.

With time, the relation with Razan became symbiotic. He became my Mephisto, my Cayor worm, living under my skin, speaking through me. Razan became the devil that the militia thug who borrowed my notebook had been trying to prevent from entering our classrooms and our minds.

But it was too late.

With time, my pact with Razan started to appear like the dogma of some political party or a surrealist group. Graduation from AUB was near, and plans to move on and pursue other studies required recommendation letters, good grades, and all kinds of compromises that conflicted with the thug philosophy that we were practicing. We needed to go underground, change our ways, and develop new ones. Perhaps there is a way to deconstruct here and queer there without cutting people off in cars or dragging them to dungeons or living rooms to be tried and roughed up. Even my childhood friend and his first love were forced to compromise, take a break, which eventually doomed their relationship.

Razan and I broke apart at the beginning of 2001. I was feeling burned out from theory and the philosophy of action. It was time for me to give up on the thuggery that we had inherited from the civil war,

that gave West Beirutis a special pride in their savagery, no matter how many languages they spoke. It
was hard for me to disown the lesson that the thug
who came asking for my notebook taught me as well.

I had to move on. Demons were coming to me at
night, burrowing in my guts, and neither the thug of
philosophy nor Razan could protect me from them.

The dungeons and rat-infested basements had now
overtaken my bedroom, and I needed to confront
them on my own.

11

AN EERIE CANAL

I got a new office overlooking the main quad. It was time to cull, unpack my library. What books can continue the journey with me from Beirut to Abidjan, upstate New York to New York City, and from Austin to Hanover? As I was going over my theory books, I picked up one about ghosts, the end of the Cold War, and the return of the repressed. But as I pulled it off the shelf, a note fell out.

The note was a short paragraph describing a condition called delusions of parasitosis, also known as delusional infestation. When this rare condition afflicts patients, they become convinced that insects have infested their surroundings, crawling on their skin. Doctors report that patients pick at their skin to produce samples. They may pick up scabs or lint or other items that they consider to be the parasite devouring them.

After I found the note, I looked up its origin, and discovered that it was a photocopy from the fourth edition of *Diagnostic and Statistical Manual of Mental Disorders (DSM)*, from the section on psychotic disorders.

The note was an old photocopied page, the writing somewhat faded. There was a ghostly shadow captured in the image, blurring the top part of the page but leaving the paragraph intact. One could surmise that the copy had been made in haste, on an old copier, in a doctor's office in the late nineties. The copy was taken by the doctor himself, in between patients, toward the end of the day, in an office complex overlooking Cayuga Lake, in Ithaca, upstate New York.

It must have been dark that day, a winter day no doubt, turning the spacious yet dimly lit office into something akin to a classroom, or one of those rooms used for AA meetings. There was no exam table or scale or blood pressure monitor. The patients came to that room to share, looking for someone to believe them, to acknowledge a pain that kept them from sleeping.

The patients spoke of little creatures that came to them under the cover of darkness, so that no one could witness their assault. They even brought evidence of the nightly raids: bits of lint—cocoons of agony.

The patients came to tell their stories, to plead with the doctor to look further, deeper, to send the samples out to labs with sophisticated microscopes that might finally uncover the perpetrators' identity. They spoke nervously. Their jittery speech carried the vibrations of those monstrous drills with which the creatures were poking at their skin at night. They spoke hastily, with their heartbeat reaching speeds and crescendos that would have made the blood pressure monitor burst and break. They were like the survivors of catastrophic events, such as wars and genocides, that were never covered by any media and were now forgotten.

The patients came to the doctor's office in a solemn procession, offering bits and pieces of their own flesh. They were exhausted, drained, desperate to make a last stand against the forces of darkness. They were anxious to get rid of those spirits that one could find in *The Arabian Nights* and in the narratives of the possessed, who seek out mediums and witch doctors for exorcism and amulets. But what these patients would eventually realize is that to make the drilling stop, or learn how to live with it, they needed to enter those portals that were now opening on their lacerated skin. They needed to pull at the thread of their cocoons, unwrap them, and retrieve a long history of separation and displacement.

The forgotten note from the *DSM*'s section on psychosis was a ticket to a journey inside my body, into my deepest past.

The suitcase was too big. The lady at the check-in counter refused to let it through. She was adamant. I had to wait while my mom and her friend who were accompanying me to the airport that day went to the bag sellers in a nearby neighborhood to buy me two medium-sized bags. But I wanted the big one. I wanted all my belongings to travel together. I wanted a suitcase in which I could fit, a suitcase that I wished my brothers and sister had when they left for the U.S. for the first time to reunite with their mother. I wished that they had a large suitcase like this one, so that I could sneak into it at night, without them seeing me, without them wanting to take me. No need for oxygen tanks and special operation commandos to travel in this suitcase. All that one needs is to get into a fetal position and receive nourishment from the tightly packed clothes and books.

The books that accompanied me on my journey to America that day included Baudelaire's *The Flowers of Evil*, Sade's *Philosophy in the Bedroom*, Camus's *The Rebel*, and Freud's *Civilization and Its Discontents*.

I still remember the big suitcase that never made it across the ocean that day. It was a large, maroon leather bag with four golden wheels and a pulling strap on the side. I had found it in the attic when preparing for the trip. I cleaned it myself and got the leather to shine and the gold wheels to glitter. It was going to be a capsule that would eject and transport me to another planet, another dimension.

I needed this big suitcase to fit all my books and oversized clothes. By that time, my father had died, and shopping in London's department stores was a thing of the past. I was surviving mostly on used clothes and gifts from family and friends. I had to take what I was offered, with no fitting sessions or tryouts for width and length.

I had a turquoise sweater with a curved collar and a striped wool shirt that had been damaged and then patched up. I remember a pair of loafers that I had gotten from Hamra Street. They were so big that it was hard to walk or go up the stairs in them. There was also my ultimate companion for years to come: a black leather jacket that was a size or two too big. The jacket was bulky and crushed my shoulders, but it was going to protect me from the cold and loneliness of upstate New York.

The clothes I wore as a teenager were all too big. But I was going to outgrow them, I thought, and grow taller and taller and taller. So when I first got to America, I started buying secondhand clothes that were too big as well. I fell in love with consignment stores. Their clothes were like hand-me-downs from strangers with whom I now had a connection, just like my brothers. I felt right at home.

Eventually, I gave up on the idea of growing and rebelled against my own clothing regimen. I went to the other extreme. I started buying pointy shoes that hurt my feet and tight pants and shirts that scraped my skin. My body had to be packed tightly, like those books and clothes in that big suitcase that I wanted to bring to America that day.

I was leaving Lebanon for good. I asked the driver to take the long way to the airport, along the beachfront, so I could encircle the city one last time, so I could imprint my mind with the view of the sea. I wanted to inhale its smell and preserve it within me. That smell, which impregnated my entrails on that day in August, would gestate and rise again every summer, tickling my nostrils and connecting me to the place I left behind.

I close my eyes and start smelling the algae at low tide, baking in the sun. Green and purple algae wrapped around the rocks like lace and tassel, revealing the holes and crevices where crab and fish seek shelter from the predators of the open sea. The algae and seaweed eggs generate a special kind of pheromones called dictyopterenes. These pheromones turned me into a creature of the sea, into a creature of desire, answering their mating call every summer, no matter where I am or whom I'm with. The smell of the sea rises within me, takes hold of my body, and makes me feel as if the water were splashing me again, leaving little white crystals on my skin once the salt dries out.

Every summer, I start smelling the Beirut Sea. Every summer, I start feeling the pointy rocks poke at my feet as I head out to jump into the deep. The pain that I feel when walking on the rocks with bare feet and the seaweed smells of the Beirut Sea are the ingredients of my sensuous being. They reward me for reuniting with them and punish me for replacing them with other smells and bodies of water.

A few weeks after my arrival upstate, I was invited by a couple of friends to go sailing on Lake Ontario. We picked up sandwiches and drinks and headed up to the lake. It was a cold and cloudy day, nothing compared to the seascape I had left behind. As the small sailboat was cutting through the waves on the windy lake, I began to feel nauseated. I stuck my head out to the side and the food and whatever else was in those entrails started gushing out.

It was like that scene from *Brokeback Mountain* when Ennis broke down after Jack drove away.

In the summer of 1994, I came to the U.S. to start my graduate studies at the University of Rochester. It was the same year that the *Day Peckinpaugh*, a commercial ship that transported goods up and down the Erie Canal, was retired. The canal, which encroached on and divided the Oneida and Onondaga territories, among others, and led to the tribes' displacement, contributed to the wealth and prosperity of Rochester and other cities upstate. It connected Lake Erie and the other Great Lakes farther west to the Hudson River and the Atlantic Ocean. When it opened in 1825, the canal was considered an engineering marvel, the second longest in the world after the Grand Canal of China. It was the superhighway of the nineteenth and twentieth centuries. It led cities like Buffalo, Syracuse, Utica, Rome, and Rochester to rise and thrive.

Many of the Lebanese immigrants who started arriving in Ellis Island in the second half of the nineteenth century ended up moving to the cities on the canal. There were streets and avenues that carried Arabic names like "Abdallah," markers of a community that had once prospered.

By the time I arrived, developments in transportation technology and the age of globalization and outsourcing were decimating these towns. Gradually, the region would lose much of its population. Its stately buildings were transformed into memorials for a gilded age that was long gone. I used to drive through these upstate towns, thinking that their inhabitants must have suddenly abandoned them. Beautiful houses were now withering from the cold and moisture of harsh winters, shuttered with "For Sale" signs that had been placed there long ago. I was discovering a different kind of devastation from the one I knew. It was an economic devastation that I would see repeatedly in American cities in Pennsylvania, New York, New Hampshire, and elsewhere. People packing their most valuable belongings in one big suitcase and moving on to escape poverty, loneliness, death.

Rochester was the headquarters of companies like Bausch & Lomb, Xerox, and, of course, its crown jewel, Eastman Kodak. Kodak made the cameras and film used to document my childhood. Kodak has been with me since I was born, since my first pose in front of the camera, and now I had come to find its source in Rochester.

With its companies producing the most advanced visual technology, from lenses and cameras to photocopiers and film, Rochester was the cradle of the image. I suddenly found myself in the shoes of those explorers who seek out the origins of culture and civilization, to understand something about who they are and where they come from. Without meaning to do so, I found myself reversing those explorers' journeys, as they searched for the source of the Nile or of the pyramids' entrance. I was moving from East to West, from the wilderness that Job, Hagar, and other prophets and saints inhabited to the frigid wilderness of upstate New York, which held the key to how images are formed and how memory is recorded.

The imaging companies in Rochester anticipated the catastrophe that would befall the cities on the Erie Canal. It was as if they were developing the tools to capture these cities' demise and to expose it both in museums and in real time to the new immigrants who followed in the footsteps of their predecessors. For a kid who thought he was escaping war, I soon realized that it was all around me, reenacted in streets and squares, and on film kept in the special archives of collapse.

I was twenty-one when I arrived in Rochester. A friend in Beirut knew someone who was studying there and had said that it was a good school, so I applied. I applied to a few other schools as well that people had recommended for comparative literature, the field that was going to allow me to combine my love for philosophy with that of literature, languages, and visual arts.

I went to the Beirut office of Amideast, an American organization founded in 1951 to foster cultural and educational exchange with the region. Their office was on Makdisi Street, by the AUB. A receptionist directed me to a big book of American universities. It was a Kaplan guide, listing basic information about each institution, including features and mailing addresses. When I opened that book, I was transported into a world from which I have not yet emerged.

A few weeks after mailing out inquiry letters, brochures started pouring in, displaying pictures of historic buildings and green lawns, and listing courses and subjects that aroused my curiosity. The University of Rochester accepted me and offered me a full scholarship, and, as I later discovered, a teaching assistantship with a modest stipend. Little did I know when I applied that Rochester had a cutting-edge program in visual and cultural studies and comparative literature, with scholars teaching courses on psychoanalysis, feminism, film, race, queer theory, and deconstruction. I lucked out. I was finally going to discover the theories behind my performances of gender and sexuality, and the limits of theory in accounting for them.

But because I was moving from an exam-heavy system to a seminar-paper one, I struggled with writing. By the end of my first year, I had four incompletes. I felt guilty, ashamed, as if owing money to various creditors that I couldn't pay back. Finally, one of the students whom I had befriended sat me down and helped me edit a paper on Jean-Luc Godard's film *Masculin Féminin*. He went over it with me, line by line, editing and explaining his various changes. He taught me how to write academic papers, how to write clearly and succinctly, and connect, connect, connect. I later published my paper on Godard and used it as a writing sample to continue my journey from Rochester to Ithaca, where I got a PhD from Cornell.

The people I met at Rochester all doted on the little kid from Beirut, who had a critical mind and a mischievous streak. They drove me around, helped me move, and even took me out dancing to the tunes of funk and pop and Madonna's music. And while her song "Express Yourself" was a wink to the winds of change sweeping the world at the end of the eighties, her "Human Nature," which came out the year I arrived in Rochester, was a comfortable moment in that purely, exquisitely American decade.

It's not necessary to stop at expressing yourself, the message went, now you can dig deep into your darkest fantasies without feeling ashamed.

While the winners of the Cold War were still basking in their victory, they were gradually losing their warrior ethos. We moved in the midnineties to Sacher-Masoch and *Venus in Furs*. This is what happened to the aristocracy in Europe, starting in the seventeenth century if not before. They had been retired from the battlefield and relegated to the bedroom. There, they practiced debauchery and fought enemies that lay deep within. This was bound to have also happened to the fighters of the Lebanese Civil War that had just ended. And though the AIDS epidemic was still raging, I was eagerly exploring the depths of that human nature for which one needn't be sorry, as Madonna says.

When I first saw it in the window of the Salvation Army next to my house, I felt a visceral pull in my gut. It was a patchwork of white, gray, brown, and black fur. It resembled the coat that Glenn Close wore for her role as Cruella de Vil, except it was little rabbits rather than Dalmatians who had been sacrificed to make the coat that was pulling me that day. It was plush and fluffy and came down to the knee. Price tag: $40.

When I went into the store, I discovered a whole rack of them, all the way in the back, pleading with me to take them in, to protect them from the cold of the harsh Rochester winters. The rack united the animal kingdom, with coats made from beaver, rabbit, and fox. There were fox collars with a clip that attached the two animals and reunited them in death. I felt like Jason in this temple of fur, deciding which golden fleece to bring home.

On her first trip to the U.S., in the early eighties, my mom bought a black mink coat that she wore only once. But I was obsessed with this coat. I was fascinated to discover this sublime object, shiny, alive, brought to Beirut like a trophy of war. I wore it once to a Halloween party. She was traveling at the time and never found out. I wore it with nothing underneath, or maybe some underwear or stockings. Who needs clothes when I am enveloped in fur, in my mother's skin? So when I saw the fur coats at the Salvation Army and at other consignment stores in Rochester, I gasped, I went insane. I started pleading with the gatekeepers of these shops to let me buy them for a discount. They were already cheap, but I had so little money and such a great craving that I bargained my way into this paradise of fur. I started collecting them, one by one, enveloping myself in them, imagining my mom wrapping herself around me.

In the end, I had over thirty coats. They crossed styles and gender and occupied all my closet space and the most intimate place in my heart. I wore them to school, to dinner parties, to bars, everywhere. The biggest fans of my fur coats were homeless people. It was no surprise that they, too, appreciated these sublime objects. They, too, understood the wandering and cold that we expected these pelts to protect us against.

Eventually, I had to let go of my fur coats. All except one, all except the patchwork coat with the little rabbits that I had first laid my eyes on in that store window on Monroe Avenue.

In Rochester, there were times when I was so lonely that I would take out my contacts list and start dialing people I knew or whose numbers had been given to me when I left Beirut. There were relatives in California, friends in DC, aunts, cousins, and acquaintances all over. It didn't matter whom I called, as long as I called, as long as I felt connected to someone who carried the whiff of home. I would start with the long-distance calls—which cost money at the time— and then gradually make my way to the international ones. I spent most of the money that my brothers sent me and that I earned as a teaching assistant on phone calls. I was the dutiful son who, no matter how far he went, kept calling, inquiring, checking in.

"E.T. phone home."

It didn't matter where I lived or how long I had been absent, these calls brought home to me. They also prevented me from making home in those places

I was moving to from upstate New York to wherever I ended up. Hours on the phone sustained a vast network of family and friends and interlocutors. This was my community, no matter how big or small was the apartment I was living in, no matter how far or isolated or cold was the town I was destined to inhabit.

Since I was spending most of my income on phone calls and fur coats, when it came time to move from my dorm room to an apartment downtown, I couldn't afford to buy a mattress. One of the students offered me her old futon. She had a black dog who used to jump and lie on that futon. She carried the futon with her boyfriend and placed it in my bedroom on the floor. I now had my own place, with my own mattress. I could finally entertain and walk to the bars and clubs nearby, every night if I wanted to.

After sleeping on the old futon for a few nights, I started waking up in the middle of the night feeling as if insects were crawling on me. I would put the lights on and look for any little creatures that were deep in that mattress, attacking my body. I started thinking of the bedbugs that I had read about in nineteenth-century French literature. I also felt like those figures in Salvador Dalí paintings who had ants crawling on them. My skin was transforming into an animal pelt that these insects would now inhabit, and that was going to keep them warm in the Rochester cold.

Where did these creatures come from? Maybe my friend's dog had fleas that had burrowed in the futon

that was now mine? Or maybe it was the secondhand clothes I was buying, or the fur coats that were
crowding my closet? Who had put this curse that was
poking me at night, preventing me from sleeping?

I went to war against the little creatures. Whatever
was left of my income was now going to be spent on
defense—an arsenal of insecticides and spray bombs
that were going to rid me of these hellish beings. I
sprayed and bombed, day and night. I became like
a madman, a junkie, calling friends at all hours to
drive me to the store so I could get my fix, so I could
buy more spray, more bombs to exterminate the evil
sleeping in my bed. It got to the point where I could
no longer pay my rent and had to leave the apartment
into which I had just moved. The leasing manager
came to show it in my absence one day, only to discover it littered with spray bombs and insecticides, a
battlefield that had traveled all the way from the Middle East to upstate New York.

But there were no dead bodies to pile up like pyramids while their stench rises to the sky. The only
evidence of the battle were the cans and bombs that
had been fired to no avail. The enemy was hiding, I
thought, deep inside bedding and futons and pillows
and at the root of every hair on my body.

Since I was fighting an enemy that was invisible
to the naked eye, that only attacked at night, I had
to find the traces of its assault on my body. I started
counting my blemishes: the little brown one on my

left arm, the little black one on my right thigh. Every morning I would emerge from my bunker to count the dead and the wounded on my skin, inspecting the damage from the nightly bombardment.

I had to fight back. I had to return to that water that envelops and cradles me. I wanted my mom, my dad, Beirut in the summer. But no one was there to protect me from this war that had erupted again. I needed a doctor, a lover, someone who could help me fight off this scourge. I was contaminated. I became convinced that whoever slept in my bed or came to visit me was getting infected by this disease that was branding me forever.

Gradually, I moved from reading books and images to reading my surroundings, my own body, interpreting the signs that were forming on my skin. I became paranoid, murderous, acting like one of those war criminals who use chemical weapons against their own people, gassing them to death. And when that didn't work, I was going to boil them alive, like heretics.

I started washing everything in boiling water. No matter whether it could be washed or not, whether it might shrink or get ruined or not. Everything had to be melted to oblivion. I was also boiling my own flesh, desperately trying to exterminate these creatures who now stuck to me, seeking the warmth of my body. I took hot showers and rubbed as hard as I could. I began using Dial soap, which promised to eliminate 99 percent of germs and parasites and all living beings, no matter how small or invisible or alien they were. These creatures were guilty, and I was going to kill them all. I was going to cleanse myself from the demons that came to me at night, that came with me all the way from Lebanon, hiding in my suitcases, under my skin, deep within my psyche. Since hot water was always available in America, I took showers daily, and more than once. I needed to make myself pure, holy, resistant to all parasites and memories. I boiled and gassed so much that I altered the ecosystem of my body, of my apartment. I was practicing biocide. I was ready to poison myself, along with the little creatures. I was like that actor in *Jaws* who wrapped himself with explosives at the end and waited for the shark to come and devour him so they could die together. I entered an altered state of consciousness. I was seeking deliverance by any means.

By the end of my first year in Rochester, I decided to shed everything, lay myself bare, destroy the shelters of these little creatures on my body, in my hair. I sat in the bathtub and took the blade to my head, to my body. The fur that covered me had to be removed. I needed to skin myself alive, like Job in the Bible when he heard that his cattle and children were struck dead.

Job got up and tore his robe and shaved his head.
Then he fell to the ground in worship and said:

*"Naked I came from my mother's womb, and naked
I will depart."*

Just like Job, I needed to rebirth myself as alone in
the world, free of any attachment, be it kin or parent.
I was metamorphosing. To kill the monster that was
devouring me, I had to become a freak myself.
I organized a garage sale and sold all my furs. No
more motherhood. By the end of that first year in
America, I was reclaiming my body, breaking with
the place I had come from. I needed to unload the
burden I was carrying all these years and across four
continents. I needed to unbreak myself.

But how? How does one extract the demons that
have burrowed deep inside, long ago?

I went to a medium once during the war in Lebanon. I was fifteen, restless, and constantly fighting
with my mom and everyone else. Dealing with war,
desire, and the recent death of my father, I was acting
out. The séance revealed a possession. The medium
said that I had taken a shower at night, and as the
wandering spirit of a man from Arabia was flying by, I
had burned it with hot water, so he had possessed me.

Back home, we believe that the jinn and other spirits roam at night, especially around water. Therefore,
when entering their domains we need to warn them
by talking to them or shouting words like *dastur*. But

I broke the law and desecrated their realm and got punished for it.

The medium proceeded to extract the spirit from my body. Her voice thickened as she started pleading with it:

"Release him, he's a poor kid, an orphan, he didn't mean to burn you."

The spirit overcame her, turning her into Whoopi Goldberg in *Ghost*. The women sitting in her living room joined in:

"Let him go! He's an orphan! He didn't mean to burn you!"

She eventually exorcised me. I felt something moving up my body and exiting from the top of my skull. Her hand was on my head as she was reciting her incantation. Then she gave me an amulet to wear, to ensure that the spirit would not return. But I never wore it.

The amulet consisted of a note on which the exorcist had written verses from the Quran that was then folded into a small square like a tefillin, which she then wrapped in haste with black duct tape instead of the traditional leather. I was supposed to carry it, and it was supposed to protect me from wandering spirits near and far. Its multiple folds would withstand my own wandering across continents and towns and offices.

The note that my exorcist gave me resembles the note that would fall out from a book on haunting written by an Algerian Jew who had to reinvent home and belonging as well. He left Algeria for France on a boat. The sea journey nauseated him, forcing him to stick his head out to the side of the boat and spill his guts out. His name was Jacques Derrida, and he is the author of *Specters of Marx*, the book I picked up that day in Hanover as I was moving offices at the height of the COVID-19 pandemic.

After months of nightly assaults, I finally decided to go see a doctor. I gathered the little pieces of lint that I thought contained the creatures assailing me and went to Rochester's Strong Memorial Hospital. The doctor was kind and patient, carefully listening to my tale of infestation. When I produced the lint that I had collected in a Ziploc bag, she examined it closely under a magnifying lens.

"Yes, perhaps there is something here. But perhaps you need to moisturize as well. How often are you showering? What soap do you use? Where do you come from? A Mediterranean climate?"

How often am I showering? Why is this even an issue? My skin looks totally fine. Crispy clean. I am in America now. I was using the most advanced washing technology and bathing daily, multiple times. Water—and hot water, no less—was abundant here. I craved this water that burned me and kept me warm. I left Lebanon for this water to run and never stop.

For me, America was a giant hot tub in which I was going to sleep and live forever.

Over the next few years, I consulted doctor after doctor, pleading with them to take my malady seriously, to examine the little pieces of lint I carried around as evidence of my affliction. A dermatologist in Beirut who was a friend of my sister told me point-blank that I should see a psychiatrist. I wasn't sure what she meant. Why would she think that I was losing it? I was simply being attacked by microscopic creatures that were living in my bed, feeding on me at night. Nineteenth-century literature is full of them. And I come from the nineteenth century, like Freud's patients.

But it wasn't until I went to see that doctor on Cayuga Lake in Ithaca, who went and photocopied on his Xerox machine the entry describing delusional infestation, that I felt vindicated. Something in that note revealed the source of my possession. When I read it, I understood that it no longer mattered whether the little creatures were real or not but that I was suffering, along with others like me. I understood that I had company in my agony, that I wasn't alone at night. It was the beginning of the cure, which would continue after I moved to New York shortly after. There I would start another process of exorcism, which consisted in unpacking the library that I had brought to the U.S. and in recognizing all those smells and pheromones emanating from the sea and algae of the Beirut coast that lay deep within me.

———————

Unknowingly, I came to Rochester to understand something about the birth of the image, about what could and couldn't be seen, captured, provided as evidence of a disease that devours one at night. Rochester was the capital of images (Kodak) and photocopies (Xerox) that were replaying the war, allowing me to see it exposed on film, on celluloid, on my own skin. These images would reveal ghosts and other spirits who could travel across time and space to claim what is rightfully theirs, to right the wrongs that they have endured, to take their revenge on the one who burned them with water and is now trying to run away. The culprit was trying to escape, seek asylum on the shores of faraway lakes and eerie canals. But to no avail.

I came to upstate New York to witness the demise of the cities and towns of the Erie Canal that were built by those who also burned the spirits that were roaming along its forests and estuaries and grave sites. Spirits of ancestors sought revenge on those who came to disturb their peace, building and thriving where they once rested. The spirits would bring ruin upon their stately homes and haunt them so they can never step foot in them again, so that they could never sleep at night.

I came to upstate New York only to realize that no amount of fur was going to protect me from the cold that was now gnawing at my bones.

The Lebanese Civil War was over, but it was alive in me, raging in my bed and on my skin. I took it to America with me. I packed it in those suitcases, along with the other books and items of clothing. I have managed to keep it alive so I can continue to cohabit with it by swimming and snorkeling and feeling the pointy rocks prick my feet as I walk to jump into the Beirut Sea.

12

ON 9/11

When I first met with my therapist in New York in March 2001 and she asked me about the war, I thought her question was absurd. Wasn't it obvious that this was All About My Mother, as Almodóvar would say? She had handed me to another woman when I was born and abandoned me when my father died. And the constant fighting at home, and my brothers and sister who left when I was a child—as if all of this wasn't enough to keep me on that blue couch for a lifetime or two.

Gradually, a world of disjointed memories started rushing in. They must have been suppressed for the war child to continue moving across countries and languages and cities and apartments in search of a brief respite, an elusive shelter.

But there was another dimension to my therapist's question on that cold March day. She was having a Cassandra-like vision of dust and blood in which a "bridegroom" (or *ariss* in Arabic) brings death and destruction to his city. She must have seen the gods of war entering the room when she let me in. She must have seen war like a halo around my head, like a light coming out of my belly. She frisked me with her discerning gaze when she called me in and found the book of war on me. That book was going to open and engulf us all.

"Turn the TV on," said the voice on the phone. Images of the towers burning were showing on all channels. Fires broke out on the buildings' top floors. Metal and glass started melting at incredible speed, threatening to flood downtown Manhattan and my life along with it.

The voice on the phone was weary. The fear was palpable, but there was something else, a sense of confusion that was directed at me, beseeching me to wipe it out in one magic word, in one decisive strike. I was, after all, a survivor of wars and bombardments, and the voice was pleading with me to explain:

"What do these images mean? What doom has befallen us? You have seen it all before. You must know!"

It was Lebanon all over again. Except it was worse, far worse. I was in New York. I had almost abandoned my academic career to be in that city, to bask in its art and architecture, and crowds and nightlife. It was the only city where I could lose myself, where I could feel that I belong, where I could dissolve into its buildings' concrete and metal and glass, which would melt and flood on that September morning.

All I had wished for since I had moved to the U.S. in 1994 was to live in New York. I wanted to wrap it around my body like a maternal skin and inhale the fumes from its buses and commuter traffic. It was in New York that I was going to understand how I was put together, how intimacies and abandonments have shaped my desire, my longings, my deepest fears.

New York was my city, and those who attacked it were going to answer to me. Didn't they realize what I had to endure to arrive here? Have they no idea what I experienced as I was escaping those skies that never stopped raining death and displacement?

On 9/11, I was living on Washington Square and teaching a course on the Middle East at New York University. It was the beginning of the term, and I was supposed to meet with my students that Tuesday to discuss a documentary I had assigned: *Islam: An Empire of Faith*. The documentary had aired on PBS a few months before and was supposed to dispel beliefs about Islam as a violent religion.

Oy vey!

———

It takes only one phone call for one's world to unravel. The call I received that morning transported me to Lebanon and to 1982 and the images of the murder of Bashir Gemayel in an explosion at his party headquarters. And while Gemayel's assassination led to the Israeli occupation of Beirut and the Sabra and Shatila massacres, 9/11 would transform my neighborhood into a military zone and the U.S. into a country of perpetual war and patriotism that would eventually rid me of any illusion of safety.

But in the meantime, I needed to huddle with my loved ones, as we did during the war back home. So I called my closest friends—a couple who lived on Park Place, right across from the World Trade Center—and asked them to come over. I also called my cousin, who had just moved from the Bay Area a week before and was now living on the Lower East Side. She had left academia and moved to New York to try her luck at fashion design. And I went out, stocked up on food, drinks, and snacks, and got the apartment ready for hosting and comforting in preparation for an extended siege.

My partner at the time, who had called to tell me what was happening that morning, worked on Maiden Lane, right around the corner from the Twin Towers. We had met in Rochester a few years before. He was kind and gentle and patiently put up with the thug philosophy and performances from West Beirut. When he returned home that day, he looked like a ghost. The towers had collapsed as he was walking up Broadway. He was covered in white dust, emerging from the apocalyptic scene not knowing if he was dead or alive. He had escaped the economic devastation of upstate New York, only to be swept away by a storm of flesh and debris that would turn the heart of American power into a site of ruin.

Having inhaled the dust and particles that contaminated the downtown area, my partner developed a respiratory condition that would afflict him for months to come. But for now, the house was full of refugees who needed care and entertainment. He barely had a chance to shower before starting to play host and cupbearer. Unknowingly, he was going to be initiated into the rituals that allowed my family and others like them to survive the war in Lebanon.

I was horrified when 9/11 happened, but I was in my element. My war instincts were kicking in, filling my breasts with milk like the wet nurse of prophets. I needed to nourish those who were gathering in our one-bedroom apartment and trying to process or disconnect from what was happening outside. The apartment, which had turned into a refugee camp, was about to witness performances of war like it had never seen before. We were going to reenact it all and party like it was 1982.

The couple from Park Place ended up staying with us for almost two months, as they couldn't get back

WATER ON FIRE

to their apartment in what was now dubbed Ground Zero. We disassembled our dining room table and put a mattress for them on the floor. They had met at the gate of an Air France flight from New York to Paris a couple of years before. The red-eye flight had been late, so a few passengers decided to hit the bar and get to know each other. The rest was history. They became friends, fell in love, got married, and had two daughters, before they eventually divorced.

I had met the husband at Cornell, and we spent every night together during my first year there. We drank and danced and listened to independent music that he had brought from Paris. He was half-Scottish and half-American but had been born and raised in France. For his graduation gift, he asked his parents to let him come with me to Lebanon in the summer. I also took him to Syria. He loved it all. He was ready.

When the girl he met at that gate in JFK joined our group, we became inseparable. She was half–Jewish American and half–French Catholic, and was born and raised in Paris and Los Angeles. She had lived in Madrid for several years as well and spoke fluent Spanish. Her dad, just like mine, had come to the U.S. for his graduate studies. While working on his PhD in engineering at MIT, he met an art student from one of the Boston colleges. They fell in love, had children, and went back to France. And just like in my dad's case, divorce ensued, and so did brokenness across continents, languages, and religions.

My cousin, the couple from Park Place, and others like them were the community that nurtured me and that I nurtured in New York, practicing the cup-bearing that I had learned as a child. And like the friends I was drawn to in Abidjan when I was living there as a teenager, these friends were half this and half that, belonging and unbelonging to their cities of birth, to their countries of residence. This community of strangers knew that there was no home to turn to when war breaks out—except for our apartment on Washington Square. So we put our fears and anxieties aside to make room for the new children of war, keeping everyone safe as the dust settled.

In the days and weeks following the attack, we couldn't open the windows due to the smoke and smell rising from the collapsed buildings. But one of the most painful parts of the experience for me were the images of the missing that were posted at every corner, on every pole in the city. And the American flags came out as well, especially in those neighborhoods in Brooklyn where many people of Muslim and Middle Eastern descent lived. Going to Bay Ridge to get food from the Arabic grocery stores felt like a trip to an American town on Memorial Day or the Fourth of July. But no amount of patriotism, heartfelt or not, would attenuate the paranoia and the security crackdown that followed the attacks.

———

"Who is it?"

"The FBI."

"Please come in. I'll put on some pants and join you in a second. Can I get you anything? Coffee perhaps?"

Ramzi was still waking up and walking around the apartment in his underwear when two FBI agents showed up at his door. He had been working for a dot-com in downtown Manhattan but got laid off a couple of weeks before 9/11. I remember going to visit Ramzi at work downtown and going for some of the three-hour lunches that caused the dot-com bubble to burst.

Ramzi and I met in New York in 1995 and immediately hit it off. He was a francophone Beiruti like me and was intellectually and politically engaged. His apartment on the Upper West Side was a party destination and welcome center for many kids from the region who were escaping toxicity and closed doors of all kinds. And when he and his partner decided to move to New Jersey, I picked up where they left off, sheltering and entertaining those who knocked at our door.

Ramzi was a Christian Palestinian born and raised in Lebanon. He moved to the States as a teenager in 1980. Concerned for his safety, his parents sent him to live with his aunt in Tennessee. He finished high school and went to East Tennessee State University for a BA in media and communication studies. He was a techie who loved gadgets. He established some of the first email groups and blogs dealing with politics and human rights, advocating for Arab, Palestinian, and queer causes.

Ramzi's family was originally from Jaffa but had intermarried with other families from Mount Lebanon. With the rise of national borders, it became difficult to determine who belonged where and to which nationality. The creation of the State of Israel and the Palestinian Nakba in 1948 turned the parents into refugees in Lebanon. They resided in Ras Beirut, the same neighborhood as AUB. During the civil war, Ras Beirut became part of West Beirut, "the Muslim sector," further complicating the fault lines of identity and belonging.

Being Palestinian, Ramzi's family lived on the "right" side of the demarcation line. All the revolutionary forces and the international Left that had descended on the city were there as well, supporting the Palestinian struggle and fighting against fascism and imperialism. But one day, Ramzi heard a knock at the door. It was a militiaman with a gun in his hand and a message to deliver: "What are you bourgeois Christian spies doing in our neighborhood? Get out now!"

It didn't take long for Ramzi's family to pack and move to the East, thinking that their Christian identity would serve them better in the other sector of town. That belief was quickly dispelled when another knock at the door by another militiaman with another gun delivered the same message: "You Palestinian spies, you pan-Arab leftists, get out of our neighborhood!"

There was simply no room for Ramzi's family and for their complex identities and backgrounds in Lebanon during the civil war. They had to leave, immigrate, go to America. The knock at Ramzi's door on 9/11 came from the FBI. But what was the identity or ideology that made Ramzi suspect? Was it because he was originally Palestinian? Lebanese? Muslim by association? The agents had gotten a report about his activities online. Some messages on a listserv about Palestine or Lebanon in which he expressed too much solidarity. So he proceeded to explain to the agents who he was and where he came from and what gender and sexuality he practiced. They must have been baffled. They must have given up trying to understand. They left him alone and never bothered him again.

9/11 brought war back to my city. It wasn't just the violent attacks, the devastation downtown, or the dead and the missing, but that suddenly we all had to explain how we fit into a simple algorithm of identity. This algorithm made no room for all the things that Ramzi and I and our community of strangers were or didn't care to be. Suddenly, the checkpoints of the Lebanese Civil War that monitored sect and belonging and determined life and death had come back, knocking at our door in the morning. These checkpoints have followed us here, courtesy of the bin

Ladens of the world and those who enable and exploit their actions. Suddenly, all the travel and displacement that brought me from Beirut to Abidjan, London to New York, seemed useless, completely unnecessary.

With time, I realized that no country or city or job could ever provide me with the security I craved. No matter my status and position or the passport I hold, the quest for a shelter had become completely futile.

9/11 awakened me that morning in our apartment in New York to the images of the burning towers and awakened the world from the utopia of globalization and the end of the Cold War and the open borders and open arms of the 1990s. It forced people like Ramzi and me to assume an identity of Arab and Muslim and Middle Easterner that was always complicated, always fragmented, and for good reason. The francophone academic performing gender and sexuality across four continents was now drawing to its end. I could no longer turn to Freud and Camus to explain where I came from and who I was.

I had to reinvent myself as Muslim and Arab, but I was going to do it my way.

The call I received that morning would put my identity and academic training in question, forcing me to come clean about being from that part of the world and to confront it in my work, no matter how enamored I was with French literature and theory. I now needed to approach the Middle East as a place of belonging, as a political entity in America, and as a subject of academic inquiry. I had to face it all on the couch, at home, and in the classroom.

I never met with my students that afternoon on 9/11. But when we reconvened a week later, the class turned into a therapy session, with students sharing their experiences and anxieties, and mourning the people they had lost. In that moment in class, I was a survivor like them, a New Yorker who experienced this tragedy firsthand, with a partner who couldn't stop coughing and with refugees in the house.

Gradually, this experience taught me how to teach the Middle East and to talk about Islam, how to read literature, and how to relinquish the fight for positive representation in a propaganda war that only entertains two positions: defense and offense, with us and against us. My career as a scholar of the region—and a scholar, period—started in that classroom, a week after 9/11.

I had to develop new theories and philosophies that would allow me to understand breakdown and collapse and the psychosomatic conditions that afflict war survivors and disoriented travelers. I was observing this breakdown in texts and images but also experiencing it myself. The invisible creatures assailing my skin at night, transforming my bedroom into a theater of war, needed to be identified as well, not by some microscope in a lab or in a doctor's office, but as characters in a play about a war child's journey across four continents. The journey meanders through languages and locales, shaping and molding the war child, and ridding it of any claim to authenticity and fixed identity.

The Arab and Muslim that I was going to become was the product of this journey and of the desires that it fosters.

I don't fit your stereotype, nor do the authors and artists and characters that I write about and discuss in class.

I declared war on those binaries that could never account for the community of strangers to which I proudly belong. In fact, I vowed to hack them and leak their secrets and hang them dry. To do so, I had to look inward and find the entrance to those portals and hallways that lead to beautiful gardens.

When I returned to my therapist's couch after 9/11, I started the process of unearthing the war experience. I finally understood her question about the war, from when we first met. She was going to play medium and ob-gyn, trying to deliver war from an obstinate womb in between my blue couch and her Eames chair.

Gradually, I started recognizing how wars and tragedies have turned me into a subject on the run, constantly moving across cities and relationships, and homes and offices. I was like a character in a video game that must at every stage find the keys to the door before the house catches fire. Time is of the essence.

The longer I stay in that house, the more unsafe I feel, and the more imminent danger becomes. And the minute I escape and find a new one, the preparation to move gets underway immediately, frantically.

9/11 exposed my modus operandi of living under fire. It exacerbated my need to occupy and vacate as many houses and offices as possible and participate in as many races as possible. Run, run, and never stop! The war survivor is programmed to compete in these tournaments, to look away from the ruin within, for there are no shelters on the horizon. Every second counts. War is all around. Run until you can't run anymore, until you crash and break down. Let go of love and focus on work and you'll be saved. Leave New York and your loved ones like Lot did, and never look back. Every city is a potential Sodom and Gomorrah. Run and compete and get the accolades that make you forget and bear the pain of separation and loss.

After 9/11, I ran and competed and never looked back. The itching stopped. I don't know how it stopped, but it did. No worms trying to inhabit my flesh anymore. I became inhospitable to these little creatures. Perhaps I forgot about them and stopped being sensitive to their tiny incisions.

I understood with time that there are other ways that we register pain and deal with the ghosts that assail us at night. Pain is something we live with, we forget about. There is no healing and absolution, there is no putting the patient back together, as I had imagined when I first set foot in my therapist's office on the Upper West Side. Only tricks and games allow us to survive—an endless cycle of hide-and-seek on the ruins of Atlantis.

To survive, I had to learn to cohabit with war, to be like water, from the beach of Beirut to wherever I am now. I had to accept that water burns and keeps me warm, that war is a traumatizing experience and a way of life.

The bullet of war lives in my head, inhabits my entrails. I resent it yet cradle it at the same time. I have inherited war's monstrous traits and learned to comfort its victims.

The child of war can never leave his mother behind. He simply grows up, caring for war like an aging parent. He must preserve it, embrace it as he falls asleep, keeping it warm on those cold winter nights. He returns it to his womb, in his belly, where no intruders can ever find it or awaken it in the night. There, they become one.

But when the morning sun rises, children always come out to play.

WORKS CITED

4   "The *Agamemnon* of Aeschylus." Translated by Louis MacNeice. In *Classics in Translation, Volume I: Greek Literature*, edited by Paul MacKendrick and Herbert M. Howe, 147. Madison, WI: The University of Wisconsin Press, [1952] 1980.

30   *Sahih al-Bukhari* 2264. Translated by Dr. Muhsin Khan. https://sunnah.com/bukhari:3364

31   Homer. *The Iliad*. Book XX. Translated by A. S. Kline, copyright © 2009.

32   "Ibn Zuhr." In *Hispano-Arabic Poetry: A Student Anthology*. Translated by James T. Monroe, 288. Piscataway, NJ: Gorgias Press, 2004.

33   Gérard de Nerval. *Journey to the Orient* (1851). Translated by Conrad Elphinstone, 358. New York: Antipodes Press, 2012.

64   C. F. Volney. *The Ruins, or Meditation on the Revolution of Empires and the Law of Nature*, 46. New York: Peter Eckler, 1890.

116   Pliny the Elder. "Syria." In *Natural History*, volume V, chapter 13. Translated by John Bostock and Henry Thomas Riley. London: H. G. Bohn, 1855.

122   Elias Abu-Shabaki. "The Sower." In *Al-Alhan* (Melodies) (1941), 14. London: Hindawi, 2017. Translated by the author.

135   Leon Dash. "Israeli Forces Inch Forward in West Beirut." *Washington Post*, August 7, 1982.

137   Mahmoud Darwish. *Memory for Forgetfulness: August, Beirut, 1982*. Translated by Ibrahim Muhawi, 8–9. Berkeley: University of California Press, 2013.

156   Shakespeare, *Macbeth*, Act 1, Scene 5, lines 129–137.

166   "Al-Atlal" lyrics/poem by Ibrahim Nagi, 1944. Translated by the author.

201   Fyodor Dostoevsky. *The Brothers Karamazov*. Translated by Richard Pevear and Larissa Volkhonsky, 256. New York: Farrar, Straus and Giroux, 1990.

212   "Trust in Me (The Python's Song)" by Robert Sherman and Richard Sherman, from *The Jungle Book*, 1967.

232   Job 1:20–22, The Holy Bible, New International Version.

TAREK EL-ARISS is the James Wright Professor and Chair of Middle Eastern Studies at Dartmouth College and was a Guggenheim Fellow (2021–22). Trained in philosophy, comparative literature, and visual and cultural studies at the American University of Beirut, the University of Rochester, and Cornell University, he is the author of *Trials of Arab Modernity: Literary Affects and the New Political* and *Leaks, Hacks, and Scandals: Arab Culture in the Digital Age*, and editor of the MLA anthology *The Arab Renaissance: A Bilingual Anthology of the Nahda.*